E

MW00532425

"*In this wonderfully readable book, Margaret Connor does an elegant job of capturing the essence of family life along with the customs, mores, and lifestyle of rural Ireland in the 1950s and 1960s. Hers is a life story rich in detail, history and ambition. Enjoyable and beautifully informative.*"

Michael J. Dowling, author, president and CEO of Northwell Health

"*Margaret Connor brings back vividly a time of joy and innocence that she experienced growing up in Ireland. A feel-good read. What we need today!*"

Mary Pat Kelly, Irish American film maker and best-selling author

"*To quote L.P. Hartley 'The past is a foreign country. They do things differently there'. The Ireland of the 2020s is a world apart from that of the 1950s and 60s. Margaret Connor's elegantly crafted memoir, set out as a series of themed chapters, describes the reality of Ireland in the 1950s and 60s from the perspective of one who grew up there and can now look back from the vantage point of years of life and success in the United States. Never maudlin or sentimental, it is beautifully written in a style which is authentic and sympathetic, while not ignoring significant failings. It can be read chronologically or by themes such as village life, community, education, and religion among others. Either way it more than repays the effort; I strongly recommend it.*"

James J. Browne, PhD, MRIA, president emeritus of the National University of Ireland, Galway

"*This book is a charming story on rural life in post-war Ireland. Set in County Mayo, it offers the reader both a historical and a cultural overview of small-farm existence at that time. In particular, Margaret points out the strength of the community with friendly neighbours supporting each other. Though poor and* limited then based on today's perspective, money could not buy the riches of the tradition, culture and environment. We have much to learn from this simple lifestyle as documented by Margaret, covering the innocence, civility and stability of her youth."

Niall O'Dowd, Irish American journalist and author, founder of the Irish American Magazine and the Irish Voice Newspaper

"My Ireland is rich in detail and generous in its scope as it recreates and examines the lived experience of growing up in 1950s Ireland. Personal stories like these are always valuable to gather, and Margaret Connor has been meticulous and evocative as she gathers the stories of her younger life and of those who surrounded it."

Belinda McKeon, Irish writer, award-winning novelist and associate professor at Maynooth University, Ireland

"A beautifully written, endearing and evocative memoir of family life and growing up on a farm in 1950s' West Ireland, followed by a transition as a youth to the bustling lifestyle of Dublin City and America, and a return once again to her beloved Ireland by an author who gives a moving and touching portrayal of rural Ireland."

John D. Feerick, Irish American author and professor of law at Fordham University, U.S.A.

"In My Ireland Margaret Connor revisits her childhood on a farm in rural Mayo in the 1950s. This was an era of close family and community life, united in interdependency, strong in faith and morals. Life then was not easy but had its own rewards and prepared Margaret for the successful and generous life she has lived."

Nollaig Mac Congáil, PhD, professor emeritus of Irish studies at the National University of Ireland, Galway

# MY
# IRELAND

A Memoir

by

Margaret Connor

Published by Book Hub Publishing, An Independent Publishing House,
Galway and Limerick, Ireland. www.bookhubpublishing.com

Editor: Dr. Niall MacGiolla Bhui.

Cover Design and Interior Formatting: Dorothy Dreyer.

Illustrators: Martin Beckett and Declan Considine.

ISBN: 978-1-7398725-3-3

*Book Hub Publishing uses paper sourced from sustainable forestry.

# Foreword

From the Editor:

*My Ireland* presents a factual and descriptive account of Ireland in the 1950s from the perspective of the author looking back on her early life in the country of her birth. Margaret's captivating and charming story renders a nostalgic picture of Ireland independent of the inequalities and poverty that existed there at that time. Her story concentrates, instead, on rural life with its wonderful sense of community *meitheal* (an Irish word that describes how neighbours came together to assist in a range of tasks such as the harvesting of crops). To a lesser extent, the author addresses the deep cultural divide of class and money as experienced in religion, education and professional opportunities. The book is structured chronologically, from Margaret's childhood to adolescence and from leaving home for Dublin, Ireland's capital city, and later to emigration. Beginning with family, the description of her father's passing is written from a child's viewpoint. This leads to a narrative on her mother, a unique and forthright woman for her day. The story increases in momentum as Margaret goes to work in Dublin. The newness and wonders of the city take her on an exploratory journey through theatres, shops and the banter of the street traders. Throughout the book are special moments in nature and traditional Irish song and verse.

*My Ireland* is a historical and cultural walk down memory lane.

(As standard, italics is used to aid the reader with foreign words and phrases).

# Dedication

I wish to dedicate this book to my parents, John and Margaret Connor, to my brothers, Jim and John, and to my sister Francie, with all my love.

*Beidh mé choíche faoi chomaoin mhór acu agus is buan iad i gcónaí i mo chuid smaointe.*

# Acknowledgements

I would like to begin by thanking members of the Book Hub Publishing Team for collaborating with me on *My Ireland*. Their knowledge of the Irish language, culture and history was foremost for critiquing my memoir. In particular, I want to credit team members Niall and Dorothy for their combined expertise. Next, I want to acknowledge the artwork of the illustrators, Martin Beckett and Declan Considine, who produced accurate drawings commensurate with scenes I described to them. For encouraging me to write my book, I want to render special recognition to my long-term friend, Arvin Murch. Arvin believed that my story should be documented based on the highlights I shared with him about my Irish girlhood. In addition, he offered to read and critique my written materials as I progressed with my memoir. Similarly, I want to thank Elliott Jacobson, my dear friend for the past thirty plus years. Elliott set me on the right track after reviewing the initial outline and draft of my book. With his judgement, Elliott provided critical feedback and suggestions on relevant content. To John Mace, my library friend, I extend my appreciation for his keen eye on layout and presentation. John was instrumental in shaping my memoir for clarity and design for which I am beholden to him. I am also indebted to my childhood friend, Noreen Loftus-Baker, who filled in the missing gaps on local events and customs during our day. Also, of great help was my friend, Mary Walshe, who assisted in refining many of the scenes we both encountered during our years in Dublin. A special thanks to Maureen Harrison-Walsh for her input on happenings that we both experienced while working in Ballina. Last but by no means least, is my gratitude to members of the Connor family, Francie, Orlaith, Mary, Eamon, Brian and Seamus, for their help in locating family photos for my book. Finally, I want to thank the Greenwich Library where I received much assistance from the friendly staff, while at the same time enjoying the resources of the facility. To all of you, I extend my acknowledgement in helping me document a cohesive and secure lifestyle with friendly neighbours in a supportive community.

# Contents

# Introduction

Writing *My Ireland* was a labour of love as I revisited the people, places and events that once populated my world. It began as a part-time project that gained momentum as the details and recall flowed almost effortlessly. The resulting memoir is just a window into a time and land that should evoke a sense of what Irish life was like in those post-war years.

Despite the death of my father when I was a young child, I have very happy memories of growing up in Ireland. Over the years, I have taken great delight in sharing highlights of my Irish life with friends and acquaintances who, in turn, encouraged me to write my experiences down. Revisiting in this way the Ireland that I loved has been an immense pleasure.

My greatest wish is to share with you that special lifestyle of simplicity and civility. It is a story that I believe is worth telling and preserving. Set in the west of Ireland, it describes village life at a time when Ireland was mainly agrarian and homogeneous. Our very survival depended on sharing and teamwork, resulting in a strong and supportive community. In our remote Mayo villages, neighbours learned to cope while, at the same time, entertaining each other with humour and innocence. It is in this setting that I describe the stages of my life before leaving home and the town of Ballina for Dublin and the New World with hopes and dreams. As it springs from my pen, may it alight in your ears and bring delight to your hearts.

Ballina, *or Béal an Átha an Atha* in Irish, meaning the mouth of the ford, as befitting the setting on the River Moy near Killala Bay. While the river is internationally known for salmon fishing, the town has gained much fame as home to Ireland's first female President, Mary Robinson, and more recently as the ancestral roots of Joe Biden, 46th President of the United States of America. Their legacies live on which, together with the treasures of a local historian, Jackie Clarke, reveal some of the town's highlights from the ancient Bronze Age cist, known as the *'Dolmen of the Four Maols'*, to the present. Early settlers in the area can be traced from the 14th century Augustinian Friary founded there. The following century saw two Franciscan Abbeys, Rosserk and Moyne, established in the vicinity, whose extensive ruins are preserved. Ballina was founded as a garrison town in the 18th century by Lord Tyrawley, an Irish officer in the British Army. The town incorporated the pre-dated Belleek estate with its Neo-Gothic castle, built for Sir Arthur Knox-Gore, Lord Lieutenant of County Sligo, which stands today as a modern hotel. On the opposite side of the Moy River is Saint Muredach's Cathedral. Built from local stone in the townland of Sligo before the 1898 revision of county boundaries, the Victorian Gothic church serves the Catholic Diocese of Killala. Along the streets of Ballina are a number of listed Victorian and Georgian structures of which the former Provincial Bank building is renowned. It was designed by the Victorian architect, Thomas Manly Deane, who also designed the National Museum in Dublin, among others. During the same era, the Ice House was built as a residence around a fish preservation ice shop. It now operates as a first-class hotel. These refurbished properties are among the mix of older three-to-four storey edifices, many in need of repair. Ballina is one of the largest towns in Mayo, with a current population of about 10,000 and it has remained a major centre of commerce through the ages.

My memories of Ballina are numerous, from my childhood years attending church services to my teenage years working in the town. The sights and sounds linger on, *Ardnaree*, an Irish word meaning hill of the king whose battle was fought during the Tudor conquest of Ireland in the 16th century,

Humbert's Monument honouring the French landing at Killala in support of the 1798 Irish Rebellion against the British Crown that ultimately failed, and the two stone-arched bridges straddling the Moy that pre-date the Great Hunger of the mid-1800s. These are a few of the many historical sites around Ballina, supported by the sound of the cathedral bell ringing out, calling us all to prayer.

*"…since all of us have the same anxieties, the same griefs, the same yearning hopes, the same passionate desire for knowledge, it may well be that the story of one… may bring some ray of light and of peace into the darkness and the storm of other lives."*

*Annie Besant: An Autobiography*
by Annie Besant (1847-1933)

# Part One

# Family

# My Parents

*"Love thee dearest, love thee, yes by yonder star I swear, which through tears above me, shines so sadly fair ..."*

Love Thee Dearest by Thomas Moore (1779-1852)

My father, John Connor, was raised on a farm close to the town of Ballina in County Mayo. My mother, Margaret (Maggie) Rafter, was raised in the adjacent village of Caltra on her own family farm. Both farms still remain with family descendants residing. Historically in rural Ireland, couples were very often introduced and matched based on land and money in order to continue the farming tradition. Hence, my parents were ideally suited for such a partnership. Following their simple Catholic wedding service at the Ballina Cathedral, they visited the town studio for one professional photograph, which became a family treasure for future generations. Thus, they began their married life, "For better, for worse, for richer, for poorer, in sickness and health, until death do us part."

# 1

# Dad

As a young man my father spent several years in England, where he worked on the farms with his brother, Jim. During those years, he learned many farming skills, including land reclamation, flax cultivation, dairy production, and orchard development.

> *"There will be bluebirds over the white cliffs of Dover,*
> *Tomorrow, just you wait and see.*
> *There will be love and laughter and peace ever after*
> *Tomorrow, just you wait and see …"*
>
> *The White Cliffs of Dover* by Walter Kent (1941)

Eventually he returned home and, with his hard-earned money, married into my Mam's farm where he applied the agricultural knowledge he had learned. Dad had great ambitions for his new home and farm. He expanded his territory by an additional ten acres by leasing neighbouring lands. I can recall the flax harvesting in a leased pond with many village men joining in as hired hands. With numerous steps in the harvesting process from the steeping to the lifting of the stalks from the pond, my memory only takes me to the final celebration at our house. Gathered around the kitchen, the men enjoyed much food, kegs of whiskey and jars of porter in appreciation for their efforts in the flax harvesting. Dad was very enterprising.

To enhance his farm, Dad drained the wetland which comprised less than ten percent of his land and he reclaimed the remainder for better use. At one side of his home, Dad dedicated about one-quarter of an acre for a fruit orchard and a vegetable garden where he planted diverse produce such as peas and berries and a selection of apple species. His ambitions extended to dairy farming and pork production for which he built appropriate facilities and a large water tank to serve his general farming needs. I remember seeing slabs of salted bacon hanging from hooks and understood that they were for family consumption rather than for sale at the butcher shop in town.

Dad was also a skilled thatcher for building and repairing thatched roofs. This traditional Irish roofing style was common around home in my day. By using locally available material such as straw, such roofing was economical and durable once maintained. For the thatching, Dad cultivated sally rods from which he made pins to secure the densely packed layers of straw onto the roof. This labour-intensive roofing method, requiring constant maintenance, has since diminished in Ireland along with its trade[1].

Sadly, Dad died after twelve years of married life, leaving behind four children, ranging from ages ten to four, of which I was the youngest. Although I was very young when he died, I have many vivid memories of my father. When I was a child in the cradle, he was the one to leave his bed at night time and tend to my needs. On Sundays, I walked with him to Mass and back home again, covering the four miles roundtrip. I recall sitting and playing with

---

[1] Sheila Longan, writing in the *Irish Central* on October 2020 noted that, "As durable as they are environmentally friendly, Irish thatched cottages are the products of centuries of history and tradition. While they currently make up less than 0.1% of the total housing stock in Ireland, in the 1800s as much as half of the population slept under thatched roofs."

my sister Francie on the seat behind him at Mass while he knelt in prayer. On one occasion, we ran ahead of him to Mass, ending up in the church choir where he found us. Later, on our way home, he stopped at a local pub for a pint and a visit with friends, while I impatiently pulled at his hand to lure him away. Those Sundays were special for me as I shared the experience of church and prayer with my father. Then, during the week, I watched him work the land on our farm where he at times put me up on Tom, our horse, for a ride.

Continuing to toil on the land through varying weather conditions, Dad gave priority to achieving goals and meeting deadlines over his own health. In the spring of 1945, he came down with a cold and cough following a drenching he received while working in the bog. After ignoring the lingering cough for some months, his family and neighbours finally convinced him to see a doctor. At that time in rural Ireland, visits to the doctor (general practitioner) were rare, except for critical illnesses. Our town of Ballina had just a few general practitioners serving all of the surrounding communities. For specialists, it was necessary to travel to the cities such as Galway or Dublin. Also, in post-war rural Ireland of the 1940s penicillin and similar antibiotics were not widely available. Deaths were common from diseases that today would be easily treatable with modern medicine.

Following his visit to Dr. Burke, father of Ireland's first female president, Mary Robinson, Dad was admitted to the hospital in Ballina where he was diagnosed with pneumonia and pleurisy. After some weeks he was released to spend time at home. I recall many neighbours visiting our house to see him then. Dressed in his best suit, he used a cane to walk around. Later, I observed him on front of our house as he sat in a chair, supported with a pillow at his back. Happy that he was home, I tumbled with joy in the garden next to him, believing that he was home for good and recuperating.

What I did not know was that the hospital had released him to spend some time with his family. I clearly recall the day he returned to the hospital. Not yet attending school or pre-school, which did not exist in Ireland then, I watched Mam support Dad as he struggled to stand up while our neighbour,

9

Mrs. Ruddy, arrived to help. Picking me up in her arms, she handed me a toy windmill on a slim wooden stick for distraction. As its propellers spun gently with the breeze, I saw Mam cry next to us. Then, an ambulance arrived and took Dad away on a stretcher. For many nights afterward, I continued to wake up asking where Dad was, while Mam assured me that he was in the hospital and would return home soon again. He never returned.

On the morning of Dad's passing, our horse, Tom, showed signs of anxiety. From his shed, we could hear his unusual movements and we wondered what was wrong. Later, we understood that our horse had already sensed the loss of his master. Until then, Tom knew only one master, the one who brought him to our farm as a young foal, then trained him to work on the land. They were a bonded team, working closely together in the fields. Tom spent the rest of his life on our farm, where he was royally treated. In a shed for himself, he was fed fine hay and for special occasions, Mam treated him to mashed turnips and apples, accompanied with hugs to his gentle face.

I have many memories of my father's death. Among them is the night of the wake at our house where family, friends and neighbours gathered.[2] For the food and servings, our neighbour, Mrs. Ruddy, took full charge as she busily moved around our house. Lying in my cot, my godfather, Jim Rafter, watched over me as I tried to sleep. In the bed next to me, my sister Francie and my brother John were both sitting up taking it all in.

Next, was the funeral parlour, where Dad was laid out as visitors passed by to pay their respects. Then, on the morning of the funeral, I recall seeing Mam dressed in black. On her coat sleeve was a patch as a symbol of mourning, which she wore for many years afterwards.

That same morning, I remember being dressed by Mrs. Ruddy at her home, a four-room cottage across the road from our house. She fed me

---

[2] An Irish wake is a final party to honour a deceased person. It is a celebration of one's life. The word 'waked' historically originated from unknown diseases that caused people to appear dead. Later at mourning time, they suddenly woke up. It was then established that a body should first be waked and watched over for at least one night before burial.

porridge, *stir-about* as we called it in those days in Ireland. Carefully dressing me, she paid particular attention to my hair, attaching a big bow to the side. Then I watched and waited on the road outside for the hackney car to collect us for the funeral Mass. After the church service, we returned to the hackney car for the funeral procession. From inside the car, I watched family, neighbours and friends walk behind the hearse for the entire distance to the cemetery. As the procession moved slowly through the town, all businesses closed their doors and lowered their window blinds out of respect, as was the custom then. On the streets, people stopped and blessed themselves. Men removed their hats and caps until the procession had passed. All of this activity was unsettling for a child of four who did not comprehend the lifetime of loss behind it. I did not understand that Dad was gone forever. I understood that he was in Heaven and looking down on me. But when he did not return, I believed that I had contributed towards his death as he ran to catch up with us children on that Sunday morning on our way to Mass.

# 2

# Mam

The thirty-acre family farm where Mam grew up had been passed down through the generations. Mam spent her entire life there, caring for her ageing parents and, later, raising her own family. The second youngest of seven children, four boys and three girls, Mam remained close to those who stayed in Ireland.[3] Following Dad's death, she continued to operate the farm, receiving help as needed from her brothers and their children. A strong and independent woman, most of the time Mam went by her maiden name, Maggie Rafter, which was unusual in Ireland once a woman had married. This allowed her to maintain her identify on the original Rafter farm. Perhaps her example formed my own sense of independence in life as I navigated my way from Ballina to Dublin and then to America.

---

[3] Of Mam's six siblings, three brothers settled in Ballina, the oldest brother and sister emigrated to the United States (U.S.) and the youngest sister moved to London. Mam lost contact with those who emigrated. Some years later, the oldest sister, Mary Ellen, wrote home to reconnect with her roots. Surprised to receive the letter, Mam wrote back with the opening line, "Well, have you not yet died?" I visited Mary Ellen in Philadelphia who cried at the airport upon seeing me, since I was her first family contact from home. She identified me in the crowd from the colour and texture of my hair which matched that of her own mother's (my grandmother).

Mam was a serious and focused woman. She ran an efficient farm and managed the money conservatively, but kept all her problems to herself. She worked both inside the house and outside on the farm from seven in the morning until nine at night. She also had a talent for knitting, sewing and mending clothes. She knitted sweaters, socks, caps and gloves for her four children, and made skirts for her two girls. She mastered the art of replacing leather soles on shoes, using a last and specialty tool. Mam washed clothes by hand weekly in a tub of hot water, using bars of carbolic soap and a washboard. Linens and towels were boiled over the fire in a pot of water, with washing soda and chunks of soap to remove difficult stains. In an effort to make them white again, it was necessary to add a small sachet of blue dye to the water. As the clothes rose in the suds, a pot stick was applied to pound them down, resembling the *Song of the Witches* in Shakespeare's *Macbeth*, *"Double, double, toil and trouble, fire burn and caldron bubble."* Such was the custom then, predating the clothes washer.

With her 'green thumb,' Mam planted a vegetable garden consisting of potatoes, carrots, parsnips, cabbages, lettuce and scallions. In addition, our fruit garden had rhubarb, currants, gooseberries and apples, all for making pies and jams. Mam baked bread daily, and cooked all meals on a turf fire. Food was never wasted. Even leftover potatoes were mashed with flour and herbs and fried in the pan for a delicious evening meal of Irish potato cakes served hot with garnished butter sauce.

Mam did a weekly seasonal churning of butter, using a dash churn. It was the custom that everyone who came by should take a turn churning, otherwise according to local folklore the *"Fairies might steal the butter."* In addition to neighbours dropping by, other possibilities were the insurance man, the postman, the priest, or the garda (Irish policeman) as they went about their rounds.[4]

---

[4] The *Garda Síochána na hÉireann* was established on August 8,1923.

They all took a turn at the churn. Consequently, the churning process could last for some time, given the social interaction it entailed. Mam's fresh buttermilk was well known from village to town, as neighbours enjoyed free samples and women from the town walked the distance to purchase a supply for their baking needs.

The word *organic* was not part of our vocabulary then. We simply took for granted the fresh vegetables from our gardens, the fruits and berries from our orchards, and meat from our farms. For special occasions, we enjoyed food from the local shop, considering it superior to our own and more prestigious for our guests, though the ingredients were unknown to us.

It took the current farmers' markets to change our perceptions about food. The organic trend has now spread to town and city, covering all food categories as shops compete for their organic inventory. We consumers rush with our pay cheques to buy our weekly supply of natural foods, similar to those we once grew in our own back gardens. We are slowly returning to our roots.

On Fridays, Mam cycled to Ballina town to collect her widow's pension and to buy fresh fish at the market, since, at that time, meat was forbidden food on Fridays according to the Catholic doctrine. Saturday was grocery shopping day. As was customary then, Mam selected a particular shop for our extra grocery supplies. The store owner, Myra O' Hora, kept a ledger on each customer reflecting debits and credits for periodic reconciliation. Mam sold her fresh hen eggs there to offset her grocery bill. The shop

was a friendly meeting place for women who often shared a drink served to them from the salon. Sometimes, Mam might just enjoy a cup of tea offered by Myra in the back kitchen of the establishment. After her shopping was done, Mam cycled home with a bag of groceries on each handlebar of her bike. We children, together with our family dogs, watched the road eagerly to see her return home. The excitement was exhilarating once she arrived with the dogs jumping all over her and we children taking the grocery bags into the house and emptying their contents onto the kitchen table full of anticipation.

*"Sure, I love the dear silver that shines in your hair*
*And the brow that's all furrowed and wrinkled with care*
*I kiss the dear fingers so toil worn for me*
*Oh, God bless you and keep you, Mother Machree…"*

*Mother Machree* by Rida Johnson Young (1875-1926)

# 3

# A Progeny of Four

W e were a small family, two boys and two girls. Jim was the oldest sibling, followed by John two years after, then Francie the next year and finally me three years later. We each had very distinct personalities and abilities.

Jim was a serious young boy who took on family responsibilities following Dad's death. He gave up a chance to go to college, believing that he had a greater obligation to support Mam on the farm until his younger siblings were raised. He was a model son and a leader of his peers, who looked to him with utmost respect. After fulfilling his obligation to the farm, Jim joined *An Garda Síochána* with which he enjoyed a successful career. Yet, he remained committed to home, supporting Mam financially for some years, and caring for his young siblings as a substitute father. Sociable and friendly, intelligent, and witty, Jim could tell a yarn as well as any *Seanchaí*.[5] He contributed to this art with his unique style, captivating his audience to the final punch line.

---

[5] A *Seanchaí* is a traditional Irish storyteller. Storytelling was the art of preserving Ireland's folklore and oral traditions. Such tales and legends told around the firesides at night formed the most treasured entertainment in rural Ireland historically.

Next there was John. Growing up, John was warm and kind, and made time to play with his two younger sisters. During Mam's absence, he was tasked with sprinkling holy water on us at bedtime. However, instead of a sprinkling, we often ended up with a shower. A mischievous young lad, John received much love from our mother. In turn, he frequently accompanied her to early morning Mass on Sundays and remained a loyal son till Mam's end.

John was the creative type who enjoyed working with his hands. After his education at the local technical school, and his apprenticeship with a leading building firm, John went on to form his own construction business. He began by building a new house at home, taking advantage of government grant money to construct on one's own land. From the quarrying of the stone to the final slate on the roof, John managed the entire project. This became his model house to generate new business.

Within a few years, he had compiled an inventory of completed projects, including several new houses and barns around the local villages. Although business was good and John had great ambitions for expansion, financing to support his growing business became challenging. Access to credit and loans was not readily available, and as payments were not always met for completed work, John decided to wind down his business. However, he remained active with his trade as a freelancer with established construction firms, and, at the same time, he continued to run the family farm. Creative and ambitious, genuine, and kind, John had a gifted singing voice that, unfortunately, was never trained to its full potential. Yet, he willingly shared his talent, singing, as requested, at community gatherings.

While on the farm, both Jim and John went about their chores whistling and singing. "You could hear them whistling for miles in the distance," one admiring neighbour would say. At home, they each played the harmonica as our dogs, Bruno and Victor, joined in to form an unwelcomed chorus. With their heads tilted towards the ceiling, the dogs howled out their tune, driving us all crazy, and quickly ending the concert.

Francie, the first daughter, must have entered the world smiling. It is said that one's personality is determined at birth, and Francie is a case in point. Always happy and in good cheer, she was her father's little girl. Each time she fetched him in the fields for mealtime at home, he returned carrying her high on his shoulders. At the age of six she fell off a roof top and broke her left arm. Upon learning of the mishap, Dad stopped his work in the conacre, one of our remote fields, to take his Francie to the hospital. Positioning her on the saddle of his bike, he held her there as he walked with the bike to the hospital, a distance of three miles, where Francie spent the night. Next morning, she was taken by ambulance to the county hospital in Castlebar, where her broken arm was set in plaster. Returning home with her arm in a cast, Francie nevertheless continued to play outdoors, running about and tumbling down hills and banks with her childhood friends.

At school, she easily alternated between learning and disrupting. Yet, when the teacher, spotting her misbehaviour, would question her on the subject at hand, she somehow came up with the correct answer. At home, Francie liked to wake up early and sing while lying in bed, making sure the rest of the household heard every note. Helping on the farm was not her thing. She preferred to sit and read, dressed in her finest with bows on her shoes. She did, however, like to rise up early on Sunday mornings to cook the family breakfast, consisting of Irish sausage, black and white pudding and bacon and eggs. This was much appreciated by our Mam who would return from early morning Mass to find breakfast ready for the family. Cooking was Francie's speciality, except for the apple tart that ended up being fed to Bruno. The dog bit off more than he could chew. Stuck in his throat, Mam acted quickly to retrieve the tart, thus saving the dog from choking. Witnessing all of this, Victor, our other dog, was clever enough to avoid sampling the experimental tart. Intelligent and opinionated, outgoing and entertaining, Francie went to London in her teens to study nursing and then emigrated to the U.S. as a registered nurse. Later, she earned a degree in art history at Berkeley University, to broaden her areas of study.

With just an eighteen-month age difference, John and Francie were close buddies growing up, attending local activities and exploring the countryside. They each won a summer scholarship for Irish studies while attending vocational school. This took them to Spiddal, an Irish speaking area in County Galway known then as a *Gaeltacht* region.[6] During the month they spoke Irish exclusively, improving their knowledge of the language, its history and its culture. Although John and Francie went their different directions in life, their loyalty and fondness for each other endured.

Finally, there was me, Margaret (Madge). As the youngest member in the family, I received much care and attention when growing up. I was an energetic child, and being raised on a farm with its numerous chores to perform was ideal for the release of my energy. Mam oftentimes relied on me to handle many of the light tasks on our farm during her absence. She also depended on me at times for last-minute errands to the shops in town. While I received gratitude and praise for such help, my obsession with house cleaning became a nuisance. Scrubbing, polishing, dusting and sweeping became routine for me. Though the end result was a sparkling house, complimented with fresh flower arrangements on each window, my efforts were not always appreciated.

Lankier than many of my friends around home, once I went further afield, my 5'7" stature was considered average. My personality has been described by others as adventurous yet responsible, ambitious, and focused. "You have come a long way," was a common remark by hiring managers, referring to my humble beginnings, as I progressed along my career track. This journey is detailed in my second book titled *My America*.

As the girls in our family, Francie and I have remained relatively close throughout our lives, beginning with an extended childhood. Lying in bed side-by-side, we told each other imaginary stories with associated plots and

---

[5] The term *Gaeltacht* refers to those regions in Ireland where the Irish language is or was the primary spoken language of the majority in the community.

schemes. Then in the outdoors, we created some of the scenes with make-shift houses, schools and churches. Of particular importance were our fictional countries, Germany and America, names familiar to us then following the war. Incorporated into our play, we competed for territorial rights in each as learned from the world news at the time. Our interests and dreams came to fruition as young adults, venturing far afield and sharing life's experiences in the New World. In time, our aspirations sent us on diverse paths, yet we stayed connected, reminiscing about the past while trying to decipher the present. Over the years, we have come to realise how fortunate we are to have each other's support as we journey through life.

# 4

# Our Family Dogs

Our two sheep dogs, Bruno and Victor, played an important role in our lives. They were responsible for herding our livestock, but they were also our companions. Bruno was close to Mam, always following in her footsteps around the farm. He had little time for us silly children, and he refused to listen to us during Mam's absence. Victor, on the other hand, was always playful. He loved the game of 'hide and seek' and quickly mastered it. Finding a hiding place, usually behind a shed door, I would call from a distance for Victor to seek me out. Knowing full well where to find me, he pretended not to know as he ran around, peeking his head behind various doors. Eventually, he would appear at my hiding spot, jumping with joy at his find and hoping that the game would continue. On one occasion as we played, we encountered our cross rooster in the garden. Seeing the rooster's spurs prepare for attack, Victor and I ran for cover. As the rooster flew to catch up with us, we headed for the nearest shed, tripping over each other as we turned the sharp corner and barely made it safely behind the closed door. From inside we could hear the rooster peck on the shed door as though knocking to get in. Victor remained in a state of excitement, jumping up and down and barking through the window until the rooster disappeared and we could make our escape.

Frequently, the dogs visited our bedroom in the mornings as we slept. Tall enough to reach the bed, they stood there wagging their tails, while staring at us. What a delight it was to wake up seeing their smiling faces at the start of a new day! Every family owned a dog or two for help on the farm. The dogs were identified by their owners' surname, expanding the households with dog names. They roamed freely but always knew where home was. At times, our dogs took off to visit their pals at night-time. Knowing that they should not be out late, they tried sneaking home hoping not to get caught, but as they rattled the gate upon entrance, we knew what they were up to. Next morning, their guilty faces were a sure giveaway. They were as human as we ourselves.

Part Two

# Village Life

# 5

# Caltra Village

The village of Caltra, also known as Ballyholan, is located approximately one mile (1.6 kilometres) outside the town of Ballina at the junction of the Bunree Bridge and the Sligo Road. Starting with the Downhill Hotel, renamed Twin Trees, the village extends in a roundabout fashion into the countryside for about two miles before connecting with adjacent villages. The landscape is scenic, beginning with the Bunree River as it flows along the main road before emptying itself into the Moy River. There, one could watch the salmon jumping freely in its waters.

In the summer months, my sister Francie and I spent our youth playing by the river, dipping ourselves in the water, though never learning to swim. We were joined by the Clark children, Eileen and Marie, and their younger siblings, whose home was close by. Eileen was hooked on reading comic books and a dip in the river was a healthy diversion. From across the river's bank, we could see and hear children from the town at play. Though the river was narrow, with steppingstones to cross, we did not venture into their territory.

Likewise, the Caltra Road itself was narrow. Built for pedestrians, bicycles and the horse-drawn carts, its design was not meant for the future surge of motor vehicles. On each side of the road were farmhouses surrounded by their lands. The hedges that intersected them offered convenient shelter from wind and rain. Seasonally, the hedges came into bloom sending off a perfume from the hawthorn, the lilac, and the odd whin bush. Each May 1st, we hung a branch from the flowering whin, together with a bunch of freshly plucked primroses, over our front door to welcome in summer and to banish the long dark winter. During my youth, Caltra Village consisted of just ten houses. All of their inhabitants were Catholic except for one Protestant family, the Walkers.

This family was financially better off than the rest, owning modern equipment and machinery, which they generously shared. The farms were handed down through the generations, and the average size of the farms then was about thirty acres. Each household farmed in a similar fashion, growing potatoes and grains of wheat, barley, oats, and rye, while cultivating straw and hay for fodder. The farms also had livestock, including cattle and pigs. Others owned sheep, horses, and donkeys. Most of the farms had a plot of bog land in the Ox Mountains, a distance of approximately six miles from home, where they harvested peat for fire fuel. Those years saw little change in Caltra Village. Homesteads remained intact without turnover in ownership or sale of lands for new development. The population of less than one hundred, comprised mainly of children and young adults, remained stable. Families reinvented themselves, leaving the farm to one member to carry on the name and the tradition of legacy which was of major importance in rural Ireland.

As children we walked the Caltra Road constantly, picking and eating wild blackberries, strawberries, and gooseberries as we passed the farmhouses. We had company along the way from our neighbour, Tadhg, a retired farmer who also had spent time in the British Army. Dressed in his World War One army uniform, complete with leggings and carrying a walking cane, Tadhg dropped into each house offering fists full of blackberries he had gathered in his pockets. We learned that it was best to accept them to avoid a string of curses. Tadhg also liked to sing while standing to attention in a salute. It was believed by many of us that he suffered from post-traumatic stress from his service in the army.[7]

In those days, it was rare for exiles to settle back at home since there was no work to be had. Instead, they spent their holidays there, reconnecting with family and neighbours. We villagers looked forward to the stream of summer holiday-makers, as they visited our homes sharing their experiences. Of those, I especially enjoyed hearing the stories told to us by Charles Ferguson about life across the 'Pond'. Charles, fair and stocky in build and not to be confused with his father Charlie, was astute on politics, expressing his views on various governments and their policies. From him I gained an understanding of what it was like to live and work in a diverse society of race and creed, acceptance and inclusion. For Charles as with most exiles, it appeared as if they worked and yearned to reunite with friends and loved ones in that peaceful village from where they came.

---

[7] It is reported that over 200,000 Irishmen served gallantly in the British forces during the First World War, 1914-1918, and that many of those war veterans returned to Ireland following the demobilization of their divisions.

"Sweet Auburn, loveliest village of the plain,

Where health and plenty cheered the labouring swain,

Where smiling spring its earliest visit paid,

And parting summer's lingering blooms delayed,

Dear lovely bowers of innocence and ease,

Seats of my youth, when every sport could please,

How often have I loitered o'er thy green?

Where humble happiness endeared each scene!

How often have I paused on every charm?

The sheltered cot, the cultivated farm,

The never-failing brook, the busy mill,

The decent church that tops the neighbouring hill,

The hawthorn bush, with seats beneath the shade,

When toil remitting lent its turn to play ..."

*The Deserted Village* by Oliver Goldsmith (1728-1774)

# 6

# Farming Cycles

---

Each spring, the lands were ploughed and the crops planted. Neighbouring farmers joined forces along with their individual horses to plough each other's lands. This match was important since the men worked closely together throughout the springtime. Their day was long as they toiled side-by-side until

dusk, with intermittent breaks for grub. As they ploughed, the birds swarmed around them chirping loudly while feasting on worms from the freshly ploughed planting soil.

For the potato planting, neighbours sent their children as helping hands. On such occasions, my cousins from town, Tony, Seamus, and Cathal Rafter, also showed up to help. As kids from the town, the country experience was fun but for us farm children, it was work. Yet, all children participated in the race to the finish. With assigned ridges and buckets of potato slits, each kid was tasked with planting a row. My sister and I shared one bucket of potato slits between us. Using our tiny hands to plant each slit in our ridge, we hunched over our bucket and deliberately dallied lest we be recruited for more of the same. Also, the sowing of grains was manual though much less labour-intensive for farmers.

Once the grain crops reached maturity, they were cut using a scythe. As a young lass, I helped my brother Jim in this role. While he cut, I held back the stalk using the long handle of a hay fork. This offered a clear view for his cut. We worked in harmony into the late evening while listening to the cuckoo bird in the distance and watching the sun  go down slowly. Next, we made sheafs from the cuttings, which were stacked until harvest time when they were carted to the home yard for threshing.

When threshing the grain in our village, each household took its turn, since many hands were needed for this work. The thresher and its related equipment were rented for the day. For Caltra, the proprietor of this machinery was the previously mentioned Walker family who also managed its performance. Essential to the efficiency of the threshing was the coordination of the men. Selected based on their abilities for the tasks at hand, the men worked in unison to the humming of the machinery. This entailed forking the sheafs from the stacks, feeding them into the thresher and bagging the grain as it separated from its stalk. The bagged grain was then sold to the local mills for processing, and later purchased from the store in the form of flour or meal to feed both family and livestock.[8]

Threshing day at a farmer's house brought much activity and excitement. When it came to my family's turn, I found it gratifying as it represented the reaping of our annual labour. Seeing the village men arrive, each carrying his own hay fork, was heart-warming knowing that they had come to help my family. Their masculine bodies and voices portrayed strength to tackle the heavy farm work, making me feel very secure. They were all so cheerful as they assembled in our yard waiting for the machinery to start and their work to begin. Soon, the humming of the thresher drowned out their voices and the smell of the fuel filled the air.

Inside our house, Mam busied herself in the kitchen preparing the food while I stood by to help and ready for last minute errands to the shop for necessary supplies. At mealtime, the men sat around the table in high spirits telling jokes. Many were given nicknames such as *Lugs* Ferguson, due to this man's big ears and *Monk* Judge, since this farmer was porky and in the image of a standard monk of the time. All was in good fun and taken lightly among themselves. It was an opportunity to bring them together socially while at the same time helping each other on their small farms. This was their livelihood, their means of supporting their families in rural Ireland as I knew it. A bountiful harvest brought great joy, but it did not always happen given the uncertain weather patterns in Ireland with its propensity for rain and wind. But, with no control over the elements, the farmers accepted their fate, tirelessly supporting each other regardless of the outcome.

Cutting and saving the turf provided another communal experience for the farmers. Historically, Irish people used turf for home heating and

---

[8] Here one is reminded of Irish famine of the mid 1800s when Ireland's grain was exported out of the country by the British, leaving the Irish people to starve as noted in the book, *The Great Hunger* by Cecil Woodham Smith.

cooking.[9] This organic fuel resulted from a combination of vegetable matter and wet climates. In my time, the farmers manually cut into the turf bank, using a two-sided spade to shape the sod. Each sod was then left on the bank, turned, and then stacked to dry by the wind and the sun. Once dry, the stacks were taken from the bog by donkey and cart. This was especially challenging when the bog was soft, making it difficult for the donkey to pull the heavy cartload of sods out to the bog roadside where they were built into a large pile pending home delivery.

The turf harvesting got underway in the summer and continued into the autumn. With plots of bogland adjacent to each other in a region of the Ox Mountains called Kilbride, the Caltra farmers went together as a group to harvest their individual turf. Fortunately, the Walker family also owned and harvested their turf in the same region. Leaving early in the morning, the Caltra farmers piled into the Walker tractor-trailer bound for the mountains. Once on the bog, the men worked on their family plots throughout the day.

Breaking for lunch, a communal fire was built, and a communal pot of water boiled for tea. All gathered around the fire to eat their individual lunches, sharing supplies as necessary. Often, they played tricks on each other by hiding another man's rations. They would break again later for afternoon tea and then continue to toil into the evening. On the six-mile journey home, they entertained each other with stories and songs while gaining an appetite for a real meal with their families once they reached home.

In autumn, each farmhouse hired a lorry for an entire day to transport the turf from the mountain to the farmyard. All neighbouring farmers joined in to help each other on that special day. Once again, the cooperative labour of neighbours supporting each other applied. Such teamwork is known in Ireland as a *Meitheal*.

---

[9] A turf bank results from a combination of bog, brambles and fir trees massed into the ground.

It could take up to seven trips back and forth from the village to the mountain to transport the average farmer's turf supply. The turf was piled high on the lorry to reduce the number of trips, and the men sat on top of the heap with no seat belts or other means of security. Also, the roads travelled

were filled with potholes and as the heaped lorry bounced and bumped along, one wonders how the men held on or why the top-heavy lorry did not flip over, given the circumstances. On the final journey back, the men would stop at a pub, where the turf owner treated each of them to a drink of choice, preferably a Guinness.

Meanwhile, the women at home were busy cooking and preparing the meals, served to the men gathered around the kitchen table. Such a day was a cause for celebration for a family as they watched each lorry-load of turf deposited in their yard. Later, the heaps of sod were built into a large stack as fuel for another year.

Harvesting the turf was considered a male exercise in my day, so my trips to Kilbride were few. Nevertheless, I recall the beauty of the mountain and of the bogland. The landscape was remote and wild with an abundance of purple heather, moor grass and cotton grass. Other vegetation of moss, rush and pond weed was prevalent, supported by the rivers and the lake systems in the area. Of special interest to me was the foxglove plant. Native to Western Europe, this tall, spiked plant produced a tubular flower that could fit over one's finger. This ornamental plant, in varying colours of purple, pink and white, grew wild around Kilbride. We never picked it, but rather left it in its environment as part of the natural beauty of the mountain.

# 7

# Modernisation

Electricity first came to Ireland as far back as 1880, with the installation of the first public electric street lamp outside the offices of the Freeman's Journal on Prince Street in Dublin. Over three decades later, the Electricity Supply Board (ESB) was formally established under the Electricity Supply Act of 1927. Not until after the Second World War did the roll-out of electricity take place in Ireland and it continued into the 1960s. By then, most of the rural population were connected to the national electric grid.

The electrification of Ireland brought about major changes to agrarian living. While it relieved a lot of home and farm drudgery, its implementation was very disruptive. Neighbours objected to electric poles being erected on their lands, electric wires and transformers connecting to their homes, and the ugly metre boxes mounted over their doors. Their voices were loud and clear, "A pole in my front garden," "Our thatched roofs will go up in flames." People were scared to touch the switches and plugs. One farmer made a point of wearing his wellingtons before *scutching on,* as he called it, while others purchased rubber gloves to avoid potential electrocution. Yet another would turn on the switch to locate his candle and matches and once lit, would turn off the electric light, content with the light of his candle. The shops were quick to promote electrical gadgets such as irons, kettles, blankets, and even small refrigerators. The rural folk, however, were slow to adapt. One of the first electrical items brought into our home was a second-hand radio. Large in size, this hunk of mahogany was mounted on the kitchen wall. We had limited stations to choose from, namely *Radio Eireann, Radio Éireann British Broadcasting* and *Radio Luxembourg*. In search of a clear reception, we moved the dial needle back and forth for broadcasting free of static. The radio, or *wireless* as it was called in Ireland, brought the outside world into our homes with global coverage and entertainment that opened our hearts and minds to national and international events and personalities. I enjoyed tuning into daily episodes of theatre, and forming the plots in my mind as the sequences continued. This led to exchanges with fellow listeners as we predicted the outcome of each unfolding plot. In essence, the radio took us into an imaginary world. It elevated our lives, becoming our primary media source. Prior to its availability, we depended on the newspapers for current events or whatever we learned through conversation.

*"For the Ireland of 1963, one of the youngest of nations and oldest of civilizations, has discovered that the achievement of nationhood is not an end but a beginning. In the years since independence, you have undergone a new and peaceful revolution, transforming the face of this land while still holding to the old spiritual and cultural values. You have modernized your economy, harnessed your rivers, diversified your industry, liberalized your trade, electrified your farms, accelerated your rate of growth, and improved the living standards of your people."*

John F. Kennedy, President of the United States, addressing the Irish Parliament on June 26, 1963

Part Three

# Homestead

# 8

# Our House

---

Our farmhouse was ideally located in Caltra Village, with easy access to the town of Ballina for shopping and other activities. The house was beautifully surrounded by hedges, walls and a gate entrance. It had flowering gardens in the front and to the side. The front garden offered various species of roses, bluebells, violets and daffodils, to name just a few. As people walked by, they sometimes stopped to smell the flowers or help themselves to some roses. At the side was a garden of rocket flowers, whose gorgeous scent filled the air. Our three-room thatched cottage, with its white lace curtains and geranium potted windows, was picture postcard material.

The three rooms consisted of a kitchen and two bedrooms. The kitchen served many functions. It was where we cooked, dined and entertained. Maintenance of the cottage was continuous. The thatched roof occasionally needed patching and repairing, since birds scraped through it in search of food. As weeds appeared on the thatch, we climbed up on a ladder to remove them, then filled in the resulting holes. Also, the rains caused the thatch to drip down on the exterior white-washed walls, leaving dark lines on the white surface. Repair necessitated scraping and refinishing, just like any paint job, except that this was never ending due to the frequent rain.

I have fond memories of our house as I sat next to the fire on those cold wintry nights with Mam on the opposite side busily knitting that special cardigan or *geansaí* for one of her four children. Wearing spectacles, she closely followed the knitting pattern placed in her lap as the ball of yarn became absorbed into stitches. It was peaceful there, watching the dancing flames of the turf fire while listening to the wind and rain against the window.

At times, the wind whistled down the chimney while the kettle sang from its crook with boiling water ready for hot cocoa which we made from Fry's packages. The Fry's cocoa box, featuring children of varying heights next to their slogan, "Growing up on Frys" captured our imagination for comparable growth. The porridge pot competed with the kettle as it brewed and bubbled with Irish oatmeal for our morning breakfast. Adding to the ambiance was the radio bringing us news from around the world along with music from Luxembourg. At eleven at night, *Radio Éireann* shut down with its signal tune, letting us know that it was time for bed. But the thought of leaving the warm fire and going to the cold bedroom, with its cement floor, was chilling.

While the bedrooms did have fireplaces, they were rarely used. Instead, we dressed for bed with flannel nightwear before jumping under the multiple blankets and covering ourselves over from head to toe. I adjusted to this way of sleeping to protect my nose from freezing since nose caps were unheard of. At times, we placed a hot water bottle in our bed to warm the sheets before bedtime. This rubber bottle offered much comfort as long as the water inside stayed hot. Wrapped in a towel, we moved it around our bed for warmth with emphasis on our feet. This heating method often caused blisters, better known as chilblains, from exposing our skin to such heat in contrast with the damp and cold Irish climate. Wearing shoes with chilblains on our heels was surely penance for our sins.

During our childhood years, we were often sent to bed early. Once warm and tucked under the blankets, it was comforting to listen to the lull of adult conversation coming from the kitchen, or to the polishing of our shoes in preparation for the morning, as we dozed off to sleep. Before shutting down for the night, the fire in the kitchen was raked, its live coals covered with ashes and a wet sod placed on top to smoulder through the night. Early morning, the coals were retrieved, and a fresh fire built around them to mark the start of a new day.

Prior to electrification, the fire was the centre of our universe in my home. In addition to cooking and heating, it served as a clothes dryer, hot press, toaster, iron and even as a hair dryer. Of these female-related tasks, the ironing proved to be most dangerous. Removing the red-hot iron from the coals, we held onto its handle with a rag and then dusted off the ashes, frequently burning our hands and our clothes as we ironed on the kitchen table. Likewise, drying our hair meant sitting on the hearth next to the fire and rotating from side-to-side and from front-to-back similar to a rotisserie chicken though distancing ourselves from the flames lest our hair catch fire. The glow from the fire lit up the room in the twilight as we prepared the oil lamp for the darkness. Routinely, we trimmed its wick with a scissors, cleaned its globe with newspapers and then lit the wick with a torch from the fire. While matchsticks could be purchased at the local shop, we spared our supply for greater use though the flaming paper torch from the fire could be dangerous.

Preparing the stable lamp, also known as a storm lamp for the outdoors, followed a similar pattern as that of the indoor oil lamp. Carried around by its handle, this lamp was all purposeful, providing light for the caring of our animals and the manual milking of our cows. Keeping an adequate reserve of paraffin oil on hand to serve the lamps was essential. Once lit, the slight scent from the burning paraffin had a soothing effect on me during those long wintry months.

Such a seemingly mundane lifestyle offered a sense of security and emotional warmth which I appreciated. I look back on it with fond memories and nostalgia and consider it precious as part of rural living.

# 9

# Life on our Farm

As with any farm, milking the cows and caring for the animals was a daily undertaking. The task of collecting our cows for milking could fall to any one of us children. The cows grazed on our Whiney Hill, about one mile from home. This roaming field stretched between two villages, Caltra and Quignashee, blocked by the hill in between. On the far side was a stone quarry, adding to its value. Clearing and reclaiming this field was one of our dad's most challenging projects. Determined to get rid of the whin bushes, he somehow managed to remove them in order to till its land.

When it came to my turn to collect the cows, I cycled the distance, accompanied by our family dogs. Arriving at the gate, I instructed the dogs to go find the milking cows and bring them to me. Somehow, they knew which cows to select from the rest of the animals. Within a short time, they rounded them up while I waited at the gate. Then, walking with my bike towards home with the dogs keeping step, we drove the cows peacefully until we arrived at Katie McCafferty's house. Katie was a short woman with her hair in a bun and, when dressing up to go out, put on a pair of glasses for a stylish effect.

She was married to *Scots Jimmy* whom she met while picking potatoes in Scotland. Katie lived happily with her large family in their rented cottage, where she ruled the roost, except for the odd occasion when Jimmy had a drink too many. In such cases, he would arrive home singing his native song, *I Belong to Glasgow*, in his thick Scottish accent, for all the neighbours to hear. Katie was fanatical about cleanliness, even making claim to the public road in front of her house, which she swept regularly. The cows had their target. Arriving at Katie's house, they took turns lifting their tails and out came the dung, splashing all over the road. Katie would then emerge with her broom in

the air, swinging it at the cows while Bruno and Victor jumped with joy, playfully barking back at Katie.

Mam raised hens, ducks, geese and turkeys on our poultry farm. Hatching new chicks was an easy process. But for new ducks, it was different, since female ducks did not hatch very often to incubate their eggs. As an alternative, the duck eggs were hatched under a regular clucking hen.[10] Once the baby ducks arrived, the mother hen simply accepted them as her young ones. Problems arose when the baby ducks jumped into the ponds while the mother hen stood on the bank, frantically flapping her wings in the air as she watched her children in the water and she unable to go in after them. It was especially delightful to observe them sheltering under her wings in the evening time, their little webbed feet sticking out as she spread her wings to cover them all.

---

[10] A clucking hen is a broody hen that just wants to sit on her eggs all day to incubate them.

They were her family.  She cared for them, protected them, and loved them as her own. The wee ducklings, in turn, looked to her as their Mam, to care for them and raise them to maturity.

While the boys in our family had the responsibility of taking the cow to the bull prior to the introduction of artificial insemination, the girls were tasked with taking the turkey hen to a male turkey. The closest owner of a male turkey, Mrs. Ernie Walker (related to the Caltra Walker family), lived in Ardvally, a village about five miles from home. The road to this house was busy and public. For such a duty, I was sent off on Mam's bike with our turkey hen fastened to the carrier, wrapped in a sack with feet tied and head protruding. Unable to reach the pedals of the bike from its saddle, I stood on the pedals as I cycled along, looking back frequently to ensure that our turkey had not escaped from the sack and flown away. Embarrassed by this awkward errand, and hoping that no one would recognise me with the turkey on the carrier, I cycled as fast as possible to my destination.

There, I was greeted by Mrs. Walker, who lived in a pristine thatched cottage. Slightly built and wearing a sleeveless apron tied in the back, this warm, gentle woman invited me to her kitchen for tea and home-made bread. Then taking my turkey hen to her back yard, we waited in anticipation of an immediate romantic encounter between the two birds. Otherwise, it meant leaving my turkey hen there on a honeymoon for later collection. No adult, of course, explained to us children what exactly was going on and, to avoid a *clip* on the ear or a warning to, "Mind your own business," we knew better not to ask. One thing for certain, however, was that my turkey hen was

41

one happy bird returning home.

The mother turkey and her flock of little ones brought variety to our poultry farm. Their elegant stature and colourful heads set them apart. Given their delicate nature, raising young turkeys had its difficulties as we sought appropriate vitamins for their diet. For such, Mam used the edible nettle, a stinging plant that grows wild in Ireland. When plucking the nettle, we wore thick gloves to protect our skin against painful stings that could last for days. The collected nettles were then boiled and mixed in with the meal that we fed to the young turkeys. While this plant is harvested commercially in other cultures for its rich vitamin extracts, the Irish fed it to the turkeys.

> *"Twas down by the Glenside I met an old woman.*
> *She was picking young nettles and scarcely saw I was coming.*
> *I listened awhile to the song she was humming,*
> *'Glory O, Glory O, to the bold Fenian men'…"*

*The Bold Fenian Men* by Peadar Kearney (1883-1942)

I was surprised at first to spot the nettle plant on the carts at a farmers' market where I learned more about its health benefits for consumers. This tells me that our turkeys were truly organic as we sold them at the market in Ballina at Christmas. In keeping with tradition, Mam kept one turkey hen behind from the flock with the intent to repeat the process for the following year with turkey eggs and a resulting new clutch.

Raising geese was different compared to other fowl, since they are monogamous. Consequently, Mam kept one goose and one gander for each year's brood. During the hatching period, the gander took charge by positioning himself at the door of the goose shed, making it necessary to leave their food outside. Once the goslings were born, the family left the nest for the outdoors and the water. The wee goslings were adorable to watch in their beautiful yellow feathers, but impossible to touch due to the cross gander. As children, we took food to them daily, always making sure to leave it a distance from their territory. On one occasion, the gander did attack me, but my screams alerted my cousin Eddie, who lived with us then. Hearing my cries, Eddie threw a block of wood to interrupt the attack. The bird jumped, but hurt itself in the fall, causing a slight limp which thereafter gained him fame in our village as the one-legged gander.

To support so many feedings, several pots of potatoes, the Irish staple, were boiled daily.[11] During Mam's absence, my sister and I handled the chore. It required placing a large pot, filled with both potatoes and water, on a cruck over a burning fire. Once the potatoes were cooked, we then lifted the heavy pot from its hook and carried it between us to the outdoors. There, we carefully turned it on its side to drain out the boiling water, while protecting the cooked potatoes, as the steam engulfed our faces. This process continued for the next batch. As the girls in the family, we were spared from heavy work on the farm, but this job was unusually dangerous for us.

The countless pots of boiled potatoes called for much water which we drew from our fresh well, carrying home several buckets daily. During a hot summer, our well occasionally dried up. In such circumstances, with permission, we went to our neighbours well. Also using this well was none other than Katie McCafferty, who claimed ownership of it. She maintained the well throughout the year, treating it with lime to purify the water. Arriving with our buckets, Katie appeared, claiming that our buckets were dirty with cow dung on the bottoms, even though they were perfectly clean. Katie, it appeared, was obsessed with cow dung.

---

[11] Until the arrival of the potato in the 16th century, grains represented the staple of the Irish diet. Cooked as either porridge or bread, grains, such as oats, wheat, barley and rye, were harvested as the food supply. Once introduced, the potato became the main food crop for the poor, due to its vitamins and minerals and the fact that it was easy to cultivate. The over dependence on the potato left the Irish people vulnerable, as experienced in the famine years of 1845 to 1849, following the potato blight that spread throughout the country, causing untold deaths and mass emigration.

# 10

# The Farmer's Daughter

Always close to my mother and forever at her side, I took great pleasure in watching her as she marked eggs with a puce pencil for hatching. Eagerly waiting for the incubation period to end, I watched for the wee chicks to arrive. Chipping through the eggshells, they appeared in different colours, black, red, and white. What a thrill it was to see them stand and chirp. Mam allowed me to take ownership of certain clutches, which meant my having to care for them. Before leaving for school in the morning, I supplied them with adequate food and water for the day. Then, rushing home in the afternoon, I attended to their needs. Occasionally, a wee chick caught a small worm in its neck. Treatment for this was archaic but most survived. One such chick, that I named Austin, was given special care by me. As I fed him and kept him warm by the fire, he grew dependant and began to follow me around. Since he was still frail, I created a make-shift pram from a tin can with a string attached to pull it along. Austin quickly adjusted to his 'pram', since it was stuffed with rags for comfort. However, as he grew and started to crow, it became time to transfer him to the hen house. By then, however, Austin had the notion that he was superior to his breed and was reluctant to join them, making the transition all the more difficult. Over time he accepted his new environment. Yet, upon recognising me in the outdoors thereafter, he would raise his head high, as though saluting his past life.

Inspired by my neighbour, Katie McCafferty, who kept a beautiful house, my aspiration was to make our house equally pretty. This desire satisfied my obsession with house cleaning, as mentioned previously in chapter three. Competing with Katie, however, proved to be challenging. It meant frequent whitewashing the exterior walls of our house, using a mixture of lime and water. Since Mam refused to keep me with an adequate supply of lime, I borrowed the shortfall from neighbours. The end result was always rewarding as I stood on the public road outside our house to view and admire my white-washing session. Katie also maintained a beautiful flower garden at the front of her house, and my goal was to duplicate a similar garden at home. As a result, I spent a great deal of time observing the variety of seasonal flowers and shrubs that Katie cultivated. She was most generous in giving me slips to plant, including red and pink geraniums, that I potted and nurtured throughout the year, taking them indoors from the frost and cold of the winter months. While in Katie's company I learned about flower seeds, and enjoyed shopping for them in Ballina with my spare pennies. I clearly remember the shop called Lowreys on Knox Street, where I spent hours browsing through the many packages of flower seeds before making my selection, based on the picture of the flower. Words cannot describe the thrill of seeing the resulting flowers grow in our garden at home. This was for sure the origin of my 'green thumb' in growing and in caring for plants.

Keeping the area around our house free of weeds also required a lot of labour. With no chemicals available to kill the roots, it was necessary to use a hoe and hand-pluck each one. For this I needed extra hands, and from observing the village farmers, I understood the importance of teamwork. Consequently, as neighbouring kids showed up for play, I had an alternative plan for them. One such playmate in particular, named Nan, was a likely candidate. As soon as Nan began to help, we could hear her mother in the distance shouting "Nanning, get back home and wash the dishes!" She knew exactly where to find her daughter, as demonstrated by the shower of stones coming in our direction, causing the pair of us to duck for cover and forcing Nan to beat a hasty retreat back to her duties.[12]

Maintaining an adequate supply of holy water in our house was important to keep out the *evil spirits* and I was held responsible for this chore. Setting off on my bike to the cathedral in town, I religiously filled up a large glass bottle from the tap at the rear of the church. This water, which resembled any other water, was considered holy since it was blessed at the church. It had many uses in our house, beginning with the fonts inside each door that required frequent refills from overuse. It also was used in storms of wind, rain, thunder, and lightning. During such storms, we frequently hid under the kitchen table, while Mam sprinkled the holy water around the floor in the hopes of keeping us safe. Given the frequency of such storms, the large glass bottle became something like a holy object itself from its numerous trips to the church for replenishment.

---

[12] Washing the dishes was an important chore in my time, given the limited supply of dishes, the large families and the fact that dishwashers were unheard of then. This job was the girls' responsibility in a family. It was necessary to leave the table ready for the next family meal.

Part Four

# Community

# 11

# Our Neighbourhood

Ours was a friendly house. The doors were always open, as neighbours came and went. Mam had a close set of women friends who took turns visiting each other back and forth. This tradition was known as rambling. The ramblers discussed all the latest news and reminisced about the past. For them, it appeared that times gone by were much better. One would hear them say, "Them's the times that were in it, God be with them, better than today." They repeated their familiar tales and elaborated on them with each telling. Mam contributed with her own stories about the neighbours. She laughed her way through them making us believe that they must be worth hearing. As she retold them to different audiences, the extended stories became more entertaining. Since I was usually present, I knew she was exaggerating and would tell her so in private. My remarks went unheeded, leaving me no choice but to cover my ears at the next telling. As an evening concluded following the serving of tea and food, the ramblers headed for home. As was the custom then, the host accompanied them for a short distance in the direction of their home, continuing the chatter as the family dog or cat followed in their footsteps.

For a reciprocal visit, the house that I enjoyed the most as a child was that of the Melia family, located in Behy Village. Mam went there frequently, taking my sister and me along. It was especially beautiful there in the springtime with its rows of double-leaved daffodils lining each side of the long pathway leading to the house. The aroma from the daffodils filled the air with their perfume. Living in the house were Danny and Bridgie, brother and sister, together with Bridgie's three children, Mick, Mary and Bernie. Theirs was the friendliest house one could visit. Even their dog added to the welcome, as he joined around the fire finding a comfortable spot to sit, preferably on one's shoes. Bridgie was always in good humour, joking and telling tales about the neighbours. Everything Bridgie said, Danny completely agreed with, while he sat by the fire smoking his pipe. More turf was added to the fire as the stories continued, and tea with homemade soda bread was served. The fables described the ghosts and the *banshees* of days gone by, making one believe they were real as the mind's eye pictured the scenes. In accordance with Irish legend, the wailing of the *banshee*, a female spirit, was a signal of an imminent death in a home. Such images were not helpful for the long nightly walk home. Scared that the spirits might appear in the dark, we listened for every sound as we clung closely together on our way home. This was the fine art of storytelling in the Ireland of my youth.

In addition to close friends, ramblers often dropped by our house unannounced during the waking hours. Should the doors be closed, visitors simply lifted the latch and walked right in. This was accepted as the norm.

*"The door is always open*
*The neighbours pay a call*
*And Father John, before he's gone,*
*Will bless the house and all …"*

*Christmas in Killarney* by John Redmond, James Cavanaugh, Frank Weldon
(1950)

The ramblers were always welcome, even if the family members were on their knees in prayer. In such instances, the visitors also knelt down and participated. I recall Tom Moyles from the adjacent village of Rathkip joining in our prayer as he came by unexpectedly. Tom filled an important role for our household as a metaphorical rooster. An early riser, the smoke from Tom's distant chimney proved to be more reliable than our old-fashioned pendulum clock hanging on our kitchen wall that we wound daily. For us, Tom's smoke signal marked the start of a new day, the rising sun. He was a religious man himself whose brother, Willie, was then a Canon of the Catholic Church. At that time, the rosary was the established family prayer following the Father Peyton campaign throughout Ireland. Known as the *Rosary Priest*, he promoted this prayer with the message that, "The family that prays together, stays together." [13]

His teachings led Irish Catholics to adopt the rosary as the family evening prayer. Consequently, one could hear the voices coming from a given house as the mother led with the *Our Father* while the rest of the family members responded with the *Hail Mary*.

From time-to-time community balls and private parties were held in neighbouring homes. Such events usually honoured villagers leaving for foreign lands or relatives visiting from abroad. It was sad to see a villager leave for distant shores such as America or Australia, knowing that they may never return. In Caltra Village, many of those functions were hosted by Jack and Annie Ferguson. Annie had spent some years in America where she gained sophistication in food and entertainment. Returning home, she settled in our village as Jack's wife, where they modernised their house. Living with them were the McNulty children whose mother had passed and whose father was

---

[13] Fr. Patrick Peyton preaching at an Irish rally in 1954.

Annie's brother. Of the six children, one boy and five girls, Ann McNulty was my age. Her aunt Annie believed that I was an ideal role model for Ann, as she sent us packing to the seashore with a luncheon of salmon sandwiches. Ann, with her combination of jet-black hair and pale skin, was an attractive girl with a drole personality. She and I were friends growing up until our lives took us in different directions. Annie, or *Auntie Anna* as the McNulty children called her, introduced her American knowledge to our community with the words, "You're none too old to learn." At her parties, we enjoyed her fine cooking and danced around the kitchen floor to the tune of a fiddle, played by Annie's relative, Billy Rafter. Those were fun communal gatherings, where villagers partied into the late night, culminating with toasts and speeches. During my years around home, I attended a number of those gatherings. The first of them was a send-off ball for Georgy Walker, a lad from our village who was emigrating to America. Georgy was an ambitious young farmer. While at home, he was innovative on his father's land, working long hours with his modern machinery. We could hear the sound of his tractor coming from the distant fields as he laboured into the darkness of the night. At his send-off ball, the village men hoisted the red-haired Georgy high with cheers of, "Hip Hip Hurrah! Hip Hip Hurrah!" Settling in Nebraska in America as a rancher, he returned briefly to London to marry with his childhood sweetheart and neighbour, Josephine McNulty.

Among the fondest memories I have of our neighbourhood are the Gaelic sporting matches that we listened to on radio. At that time, not all village folk owned a radio, so they gathered at our house where a standing invitation was extended to all. The most popular of the sporting events was Gaelic football, especially leading up to the All-Ireland Finals. These games were played in Croke Park in Dublin on Sundays, with a kick-off time of 2pm for the senior matches.[14] This meant having our dinner eaten, since it was served at noon

---

[14] Croke Park, named after Archbishop Thomas Croke, is a Gaelic athletic stadium for the hosting of Gaelic games such as the annual All-Ireland Finals in football and in hurling.

and was our principal meal of the day. Rushing to finish our meal, we cleared the kitchen for the villagers to arrive. Only men showed up, Mick Clark with his son, Noel, Jack Ferguson, and Charlie Ferguson were among the regular attendees. Suddenly, the room was packed and the radio volume at its peak. The commentator, Michael O'Hehir, filled the air with excitement. Known as the 'Voice of Gaelic games' on radio, his enthusiasm captivated his listeners. He called out the names of the players with precision, as he skilfully followed their every move around the park leading to the goal or the point they were about to score. We were totally in tune with Michael, clapping, cheering, or booing with the outcome. This was magnified when the Mayo team was playing, with cries of, "Up Mayo!" or, "Mayo God help us," reverberating from the walls.[15]

---

[15] The Mayo team has won three All-Ireland Senior Football Championships, 1936, 1950 and 1951. Since then, they have played in eleven finals, representing the longest unbroken sequence of loses in the history of the game.

The winning ball from the 1951 championship was presented at Behy school by Fr. Peter Quinn, a past pupil of the school and footballer on the winning team prior to his ordination as a Catholic priest.

Cigarettes were passed around, their butts crushed onto the cement floor. At intermission, tea and home-made apple tart was served. Then, we braced ourselves for the second half, cheering our favourite team when they scored while swearing at them when they lost. The result of the match dominated conversation for weeks. Some of our neighbours headed for Croke Park to support their favourite team, but for those who did not, the neighbourhood radio brought them the game loud and clear.

Our neighbourhood extended its support and charity in many ways, even to the traveling Gypsies and Tinkers. [16] The Tinker man collected the neighbours' tin cans, pots and buckets that were in need of repair. He returned in a few days with new bottoms in each, making them usable again. For his service, he was paid a pittance. The Gypsies, however, begged for their living. Usually women, they arrived with children in tow and offered prayers for food. These wandering people did not attend school or church. They moved from village to village, camping along the roadside either in tents or in caravans. By law, they were limited to a few days in a given spot, due to the perceived mess and destruction they caused. Many villagers objected to their presence, very often forcing them to flee from an area. When they came begging for food, neighbours might often gift them whatever food supplies they could spare. Sharing was demonstrated in other ways as well, from the service provider refusing payment for his work, believing that the money was needed more by the recipient family, to the hot tea and shelter from the rain offered to the County Council men as they worked the roads. I specifically remember the Sunday that Mam hired Henry McCafferty to drive her daughters and herself to the seashore in Inishcrone[17]. Henry's mother, Katie, decided to join us on the outing. While Mam and Katie chose to have a private seaweed bath, the rest of us preferred the ocean with the forceful Atlantic

---

[16] Theories vary on the origin of these nomads. Some speculate that they became homeless during the famine of the 1840s, while others surmise that they are descendants of the aristocratic nomads of the late Middle Ages.

[17] Inishcrone or *Inis Eascar Abhann* in Irish, means Island on the sandbank of the river.

waves. Then later, following a snack in the town, we sat on a wall waiting for Henry. Just like 'Humpty Dumpty,' Francie tumbled off the wall, grabbing Katie by the hair to break her fall. Arriving home, Henry refused payment from Mam for his hackney service overlooking his mother's painful hair attach episode. All of this contributed to a very supportive social environment.

# 12

# Social Fabric

We were a homogenous people, with religion and family as the foundation of our lives. The majority of the population was Roman Catholic, with the remaining religious groups integrated into the community in every way except for their church services. In the 1950s, Ireland was predominantly an agrarian society and large families were standard, as they provided labour to help work the land and earn money to support the household. Yet, with no birth control, unplanned large families could be a financial strain, with the older children caring for the young. Many generations lived together under the same roof be they old, disabled, or peculiar in any way. They were cared for at home until death. For Catholics, having a priest in the family to bless them all was considered a godsend. It was not uncommon for parents to encourage a son to study theology at a seminary. Should the chosen son become ordained as a priest, the family immediately gained prestige and respect.

One could argue that Ireland at that time was in some ways a matriarchal society. Women helped to enforce the religion. They visited the church frequently to complete the *Stations of the Cross* or to kneel in the pews praying with their rosary beads in a chirp-like whisper, making one wonder if a stray bird was stuck in a rafter of the church. The elderly women very often prayed in pairs, lighting candles while linking each other around in support. We referred to them as the *Hail Mary's* with their heads covered over with a scarf or a shawl, resembling the Virgin Mary herself. At home, the women ran the household and raised the children while the men worked outside to earn the money. Earnings and pay were customarily handed over to the women, giving them control of the purse strings. It was not uncommon for men to receive a weekly allowance to socialise with buddies at the pub. Permission from the *Boss* herself could be a requirement before leaving for the pub. In this sense, it was perceived that those men were undisciplined, requiring constant monitoring lest they get their hands on the money and drink or gamble it away.

Husbands and wives often led independent lives, rarely going out together for an evening. In rural Ireland there was little public entertainment to be had then other than the cinema. Consequently, the genders socialised separately, entertaining each other through interaction and conversation. Such a custom gave married couples space, and may have helped keep marriages together. Regardless, they were tied to the farm financially and bound by their religious vows, with no alternative options.

While women did help with the farm work, men tended to stay clear of all domestic duties. Most often never learning to cook, they showed up for mealtime or sat at home patiently awaiting their food. Pushing a pram or changing a child's nappy was largely unheard of for a man. For such activities, he might well be labelled a *sissy*. As a result, men played a minor role in active parenting and displayed little emotion publicly. His was a macho world and the pub was the haven where he could express himself most freely with his male peers.

# 13

# A Pub Scene

At the pub Mr. Macho joined his buddies for a pint where the *craic was mighty begorrah*[18]. Stories were exchanged about *d'oul fella* and *d'oul wan* and how they were aging nicely. Others talked about the many *Eejits*, *Amadáns* and *Plebs,* not to mention the *Chancers*, the *Yahoos* and the *Boyos* running around. Much *effin'* and *blindin'* went on about the *stinkin'* government and the state of the country, with the price of cigarettes going through the *bleddy* roof. At times, as luck might have it, a *fella* home on holidays would show up and be expected to *stand a round* of drinks for everyone in the pub, as it was *donkeys* years since they last met. As the visitor bragged about his successes abroad, some would respond, *"Is it coddin' ya* are*?"* Others might remark, *"Fair play to ya, man."* Throughout the evening, some became *fluthered* from drink but as the pub closing time approached, it was time to stop *actin' the maggot* and head for home to the wife and *childer.*

---

[18] *Begorrah*, meaning *'to be sure' or 'by God,'* is a term used to confirm a statement. It is usually associated with having a fun time.

The pub offered a sanctuary for men where they could be themselves, meet up with their pals, and enjoy a pint after a hard day's work. There, they would treat each other to a pint and pass around the cigarettes, while catching up on news and sports. It was a man's world, fostering generosity and camaraderie with one's peers. However, the social pressure in the pub, based on the concept of each man *standing a round* of drinks, could lead to increased debt and a *fondness for the bottle*, the Irish man's curse. I recall certain families around home that suffered financially and otherwise from the father's drinking as alcohol dependency was rife in Ireland then with very few treatment options. This behaviour, that women strived to control, could partially result from the lack of alternative interests and opportunities in agrarian Ireland at that time. Yet, the pub remains an important part of Irish culture both at home and abroad. Around the world, Irish themed pubs flourish offering social interaction with music and song, food and drink, fun and celebration for its patrons.

For a woman, however, it was considered unladylike to be seen in the pub in my day. Instead, elderly women joined friends in the *snug*, a small room next to the main pub entrance, where they could slip in and out easily without notice. Once inside the *snug*, drinks were served to them through a small sliding window, thus providing complete privacy. Younger women, on the other hand, preferred to meet at the café for afternoon tea and scones where they caught up on news and gossip. Amusingly, the demand for *snugs* has returned to the Irish pubs but the clientele has changed from elderly women seeking gender privacy to dating couples seeking romantic privacy.

# 14

# The Eccentrics

Ireland is known for its many colourful characters as depicted in its works of literature. It is not surprising that Caltra Village should have had its fair share over the years. For example, there was Micky and Molly, brother and sister, who lived together on their farm. Scantily clothed in a wraparound apron tied at the back with a big bow, Molly liked to milk her cow on front of their house, located next to the public road. Hearing us children approach on our noisy bicycles, Molly would dash with her bucket into hiding, leaving the cow standing there partially milked with the stool still beside her. Molly loved to collect news, but she never shared any. When entering her house on business matters, she would stand fixed in one position, moving from leg to leg, presumably to keep the circulation flowing. With each additional piece of news, Molly soaked it in while continuing to dig for more. At one point, Micky and Molly were given a new motor car by a prosperous relative. Not knowing how to drive, and not bothering to take any lessons, they took off with Micky behind the wheel and Molly sitting next to him. Turning a corner, they veered off the side of the road and crashed into the ditch. Neither was hurt, just conditioned for more spins in their brand-new motor car.

Then there was Biddy whose house was very inviting with many children to play with. Passing by, one automatically dropped in. Her husband Pat usually sat by the fire reading the newspaper, while Biddy moved around the house complaining about him. "He made sure he found a *young wan* for a wife," referring to herself now that she had a swarm of children to care for. To this Pat would reply, while looking over his reading glasses, "Pipe down woman, forever rantin' an' ravin'." In her imagination, Biddy had all kinds of plans for improving her house, including a new floor in the kitchen, a stove for cooking, a sink with running water to wash the dishes and finally a new roof to replace the thatch. Since nothing ever got done, the plans were repeated over and over. Biddy oftentimes stood at her front door, dishcloth in hand, demonstrating to passers-by her busy domestic agenda. She went to town on her bike each day, cigarette dangling from her lips, resulting in yellow lipstick rather than red. She was going to the butcher shop to buy "steak for the family dinner," is what we heard. Steak was considered a novelty for a family meal, due to its high price. If affordable, it was something to brag about to the neighbours. Biddy believed that she qualified, and her neighbours should damn well know this.

Living close to Biddy was Nell, who waited for her hens to lay an egg so that she could take them to the shop in exchange for pence. Dressed in her best coat and hat, with a feather in its ribbon representing the hen, Nell walked the two miles to town. The walking, however, caused her nylons to slip down until they reached her ankles. There was no point in pulling them back up since they were all holes to begin with, and straightening the seams at the back would be impossible now that she was out in public. For Nell, those darn garter belts, or whatever one used in those days to hold up one's nylons, never worked. Pantyhose was unknown in Nell's day, and so she was dependent on the garments available. As Nell would say, getting dressed up to go out, "is like harnessing the mule for a day on the bog."

Playing tricks on neighbours was also regular in my Ireland. For example, a farmer once took his horse to the blacksmith in town for a new set of shoes.

Once shod, the farmer tied his horse to a telegraph pole and then took off to the pub for a pint or two. Recognising the neighbour's horse, the trickster relocated the animal to a different street in town, thus causing panic as the owner staggered around in search of his horse, wondering if the animal was trying out his new shoes by hitting the road home ahead of its master.

Another occasional trick was the hiding of a neighbour's round of *poitín*.[19] This homemade whiskey or, Irish moonshine, was outlawed for unlicensed distillation. Produced in a shed and later buried in the ground to mature, neighbours might learn of its whereabouts and help themselves to the brew. Not knowing who the real culprit was, but blaming his greatest suspect, the farmer let it be known that his *poitín* was stolen. Since it was illegal, however, the Gardaí could not be notified of its theft. So, the farmer lost out on his *poitín*, while some unknown enjoyed the fruits of the labour.

> *"In a shady nook, one moonlit night, a leprechaun I spied*
> *With a scarlet cap and a coat of green, and a cruiscin by his side*
> *'Twas 'tic, tac, tic' his hammer went upon a tiny shoe*
> *And I laughed to think he was caught at last*
> *But the fairy was laughing too..."*

*The Leprechaun Song,* attributed to Patrick Weston Joyce and
Robert Dwyer Joyce (1873)

In a different situation, two local farmers got together to make a round of *poitín* in one of their remote sheds, believing that this gave them privacy from neighbours and the Gardaí. In the process, however, the still exploded, sending the shed roof flying for a soft landing in an adjacent field and drawing attention near and far. One would say that their secret plan blew up. Today

---

[19] The name *poitín* derives from its production. Distilled in a small pot, still *or pota*, its ingredients could include potatoes, malted barley, yeast and molasses. Distilled up to 90 proof, the outcome depended on the skill of the distiller, the quality of the equipment and the ingredients used.

in Ireland there are a number of commercially produced spirits labelled *poitín* or *poteen*. To qualify as legal Irish *poitín*, the production methods are regulated, following a ruling by the Irish government together with the European Union (EU). Thus, with market availability, the need for unlicensed home brew is diminished. Yet, one has to wonder if it is still possible to find some in remote Irish villages. For such folk, nothing can compare with a *drop of the hard stuff, the real McCoy, to put hair on one's chest,* and to share with friends and neighbours.

This is yet another sample of village life as I knew it with its diverse cast of characters, each one accepted as unique, and all contributing to the makeup of the community. In this setting, all lives mattered. With limited media and other forms of commercial entertainment available, they learned to entertain each other with benign innocence. They acknowledged the importance of community as they laboured daily for their modest livelihoods. They raised and educated their children as best they could, teaching them right from wrong as dictated by their culture through the generations. For them, belonging to the same race, speaking the same language, and worshiping the same God, left class as the only basis for discrimination.

As I look back on it, I feel fortunate to have been reared in such a setting. It taught me to appreciate the noble diversities of human personalities with understanding and respect. Most importantly, it made me very trusting of humankind. This faith, together with the security of village life, prepared me to venture forth independently. With cognizance, I accept the many responsibilities of life as experienced in my upbringing. This perspective also extends to my global travels where I am comfortable interacting with people, inspiring my curiosity about the admirable differences in cultures, languages and traditions, as I explore their countries. In turn, strangers often extend their welcome and offer their help.

Part Five

# Children at Play

# 15

# In Sync with Nature

As children, we spent our days outdoors, surrounded by nature, entwined in its embrace. We watched the birds build their nests from twigs and clay, lay their eggs, and hatch their fledglings. In the process, we learned to identify many bird types, their singing, and their eggs of green and blue, white and dotted. We watched them feed their nestlings by dropping a worm into their open beaks. We listened to the cuckoo in the late summer evenings, and wondered into which nest she would drop her egg for hatching by another bird. We heard the call of the corncrake from our meadow, and marked its nest in the ground for protection until its young were raised. We observed the swallows depart from our barn and head for Capistrano with their young families. The robin, thrush, finch, sparrow, willie wagtail and blackbird, among others, were ever present, sharing their song in our habitat. Our world also experienced the honey bees busy at work, the multi-coloured butterflies sucking the flowers and the frogs jumping in the ponds, their large eyes bulging out, alert for danger while in search for food.

*"Up the airy mountain, down the rushy glen,*
*We daren't go a-hunting for fear of little men;*
*Wee folk, good folk trooping all together,*
*Green jacket, red cap and white owl's feather ..."*

*The Fairies* by William Allingham (1824-1889)

Nature taught us to search for food in the wild. When we went to the seashore, we dug for cockles and mussels to fry on the pan at home, and collected seaweed, such as carrageen moss and dillisk. [20] We baked the carrageen moss, valued for its gelatine, in a mold as a dessert, while we chewed on the dillisk, rich in vitamins and minerals, as a snack. Such foods were freely available, enriching our diet with nutrients from the sea. In addition, the boys fished the local rivers, returning with trout, which combined with the mushrooms we picked in the fields, made for a delicious dinner. We plucked haws from the hawthorn tree and sloes from the blackthorn bush, snacking on them seasonally as we roamed the fields. During those childhood years, we were at one with nature, as free as the birds, requiring no supervision and with no fear of being harmed.

Certain sporting activities were for boys and others for girls. While the boys made kites and played Gaelic football, handball and soccer, the girls enjoyed skipping rope and picnics along with building doll houses and decorating them with fresh daisy-chains. Hearing and observing children at play brought much pleasure to our parents. From the distant fields came the voices of the boys playing ball. On one occasion, the boys found themselves short of players for a football match, and recruited Francie and myself as substitutes. Positioning us as goalkeepers, they assumed that between the two

---

[20] Dillisk or dulse is a macroalgae seaweed that grows on the northern coasts of the Atlantic and Pacific oceans. It is purple, red and brown in colour and is leathery in texture. Used as both food and medicine, it is harvested in the summer months and sold commercially. In Ireland, dillisk is a favorite snack food, offering dietary fiber and was harvested there historically by the monks.

of us, we could do the job of one goalkeeper. As the ball advanced down the field towards us, I focused on preventing it from going over the crossbar to score a point, while Francie ran back and forth trying to block the ball from entering the net to score a goal. We failed miserably and found ourselves quickly removed from our posts and sent to the side-line to watch and learn the fundamentals of the sport. As the football deflated with a punctured tube, the repair work took place in our kitchen, with a team of boys helping out.

Among them was Padraic who was ever ready for play. He showed up at our house frequently with his ball looking for my brothers to join him in a match. This annoyed Mam since Jim and John had work to do on our farm. Mam had a supporting advocate in this case as the voice of Katie McCafferty called from the distance, "Padraic, Padraic." Katie, who was Padraic's grandmother, somehow ended up raising the boy which also meant keeping him out of trouble.

As with football, the fashioning of a kite brought village boys together in our kitchen. This homemade creation, using rods, paper, paste and a large ball of twine, left a fine mess for us girls to clean up. Yet, participating in its flight gave us all great pleasure as we watched our kite rise towards the sky, its tail of buntings flapping behind as the wind drove it higher and higher until the attached spool of twine had reached its end.

# 16

# Trick or Treat

Both boys and girls honoured the special holidays of Saint Stephen and Saint Brigid. For Saint Stephen's Day, also known as Boxing Day outside of Ireland, as celebrated on December 26th, we hunted for a fake wren and placed it on top of a decorated pole. Then, dressed in motley clothes with masks covering our faces, we roamed from house to house carrying the pole. At each stop, we sang lyrics from the theme song, "*The wren, the wren, the king of all birds,*" followed by other acts of entertainment and, in exchange, were given money. Traditionally, the collected money went towards a village ball but, in our case, we treated ourselves to the matinee in town during the holiday season.

Likewise, Saint Brigid's Day was celebrated on February 1st. It marked the start of spring with longer, warmer days to come. One of Ireland's patron saints, Saint Brigid's memory is honoured by weaved crosses made from rushes or from straw. Many legends and folk customs are associated with Saint Brigid. It is believed that she travelled around the countryside on the eve of her feast blessing both people and livestock. As children, we dressed up in costumes and went from house to house on the eve of the Saint's holiday.

Known as *Brideogs*, *Biddies* or *Biddie Boys*, we travelled in groups offering entertainment for money. Similarly on Halloween, we did the rounds with added mischief. For homeowners who opened their doors to us, we performed joyfully. But for those who did not let us in, we banged on their doors with sods of turf. Organised as a team, we stood ready to throw the sods once our leader gave the signal. This resulted in multiple bangs at once on the same door. Certain doors were left open to protect them. This did not deter us, however, as we gathered at their doorsteps in protest. Next, we prepared for the chase from the provoked homeowner, which we thoroughly enjoyed. The chase proved to be the highlight of the sport as we ran for cover, tripping on our oversized britches and on each other while the farmer and his dogs followed in hot pursuit.

Halloween offered many other games for Irish children then, such as Blindman's Buff and Snap Apple. Blind folded with our hands tied behind our backs, prizes were offered to find and take a bite of the apple that either dangled on a string from the ceiling or floated in a basin of water. The evening also meant a search for the ring in the barmbrack.[21] This traditional loaf of bread, speckled with raisins and sultanas and containing a hidden item, is an Irish Halloween custom. While historically the items and their symbols varied, in my day only a ring was associated with the barmbrack. Seated around our supper table with the slices of the loaf in the centre, family members searched for the ring in the slices served to them. For the lucky recipient, it conveyed good fortune and wedding bells for the coming year. While Halloween was a fun time for Irish children and adults alike, it also had much deeper significance. Since it coincided with All Souls' Day, a day of remembrance for the dead, we were encouraged to pray for the departed souls who had yet to reach Heaven. This could entail a visit to the graveyard and to the church to pray and light candles for the souls. In addition, the next day was All Saints' Day which was a Holy Day of the Church honouring the saints. As such, it called for an early rise in the morning to participate at Mass in church, which also involved a long round-trip journey by foot.

Halloween or Hallows' Eve, the evening before All Hallows' Day, has special meaning for the Irish since many of its traditions are influenced by Celtic customs. Legend has it that its origins can be traced to the ancient Gaelic harvest festival of Samhain.[22]

---

[21] Barmbrack or *báirín breac* in Irish, meaning a speckled loaf due to the raisins and sultanas it contains, is associated with Halloween in Ireland. The bread is used as a fortune-telling game with items, such as a coin, a ring or a pea, baked into the bread. Each item sends a message to the recipient who finds it in a slice of the bread. The coin represents good fortune, the ring signals wedding bells, while the pea puts a damper on any marriage prospects for the year. Historically, various other items were included with associated symbols. In recent years, the only item is the ring.

[22] *Samhain*, an Irish word meaning summer's end, is an ancient Celtic spiritual festival. It marked the end of the harvest season and the beginning of winter, the dark half of the year. During the darkness of winter, the spirits could more easily return to earth. Celebrated on October 31st, *Samhain* was the most important day on the medieval Gaelic calendar, beginning and ending at sunset. Offerings were left outside and candles lit on every window to guide the souls back to their earthly homes. It is written that *Samhain* has pagan religious roots and has been celebrated in Ireland since the Middle Ages. In tracing the tradition of trick-or-treat, it is suggested that the custom of baking and sharing soul cakes may have been its origin. Dating back to the 15th century, children went door-to-door collecting soul cakes in exchange for praying for the dead. Wearing a disguise was a way to impersonate the souls, while imitating dangerous spirits led to playing pranks.

# 17

# Urban Fun

During school breaks children were permitted to attend matinees held in the town cinema. My first experience attending one was frightening. Arriving late, the cinema was dark, and the show had already begun. The film was a John Wayne western, featuring cowboys and indians at war. With painted faces and costumes adorned with feathers, the Indians spoke in strange languages. Watching them fight with bow and arrow on the large screen, it appeared as though they would escape into the cinema itself. To keep order, the usher, dressed in skirted costume and matching cap, walked up and down the aisles, shining a flashlight on the noisy children in the audience. Once the matinee ended, we were directed towards an exit and into the dark night. It was cold and rainy outside, and the two-mile walk home was fraught with fear of cowboys and indians jumping from the bushes. These fears became real that night when our neighbour Dan suddenly appeared in front of us with a loud, "BOO!"

Dan was a bachelor farmer, who lived by himself in our village. He inherited his family farm, which he continued to operate haphazardly.

Neglecting to maintain the thatched roof of the cottage, it eventually caved in, forcing Dan to be creative with his living arrangement. It was said that he suffered from a childhood illness, leaving him with a speech impediment. Yet, he was friendly and vocal. Dan walked the roads at night in the dark, and he liked to play pranks to scare us. Knowing that his jokes were harmless, we simply brushed him off by telling him to get lost.

Following my initial cinema experience, my interest in film was lessened for some time. However, great films did come to our town during those years. Among them were *The Quiet Man* directed by John Ford and starring John Wayne and Maureen O'Hara. It was filmed close to home in the village of Cong.[23] Other favourites that came to Ballina were *Going my Way* featuring Bing Crosby and Barry Fitzgerald and its sequel *The Bells of Saint Mary's*. The music from these films was especially memorable and ever present in our world.

Periodically, the Duffy Circus came to Ballina, and we children were sent off to enjoy it with a few pennies in our pockets. Inside the big tent with sawdust strewn on the floor, the scent of animals filled the air. There, I saw for the first time in real life a lion, a tiger, and an elephant. As I watched them perform their tricks in complete bewilderment, I wondered if I could train our family dogs and horse to do such acts. With Victor, I thought that it might be possible, but with Bruno there was no chance, given his stubborn nature. Tom, our horse, was a possibility, since he liked being patted and sought much attention.

Later at home, I was reminded that our animals' responsibilities on the farm left little time for learning tricks. Yet, as I observed Victor chase his own tail around in circles, I remained convinced that he had untapped talent. At the circus I watched the high wire act as the walkers balanced on the thin wires above. This was followed by the trapeze act, with flyers and catchers swinging

---

[23] Cong's connection with the 1952 Oscar winning film has made it an international tourist attraction. There, one can visit *The Quiet Man* Cottage Museum with its authentic reproductions of furnishings, artefacts and costumes, and join in the celebration with the local *Quiet Man Fan Club*.

and jumping between bars and ladders. Next were the acrobats performing their extraordinary feats of balance, agility, and motor coordination. However, what I enjoyed most were the clowns, with their white faces and extravagant costumes complete with ruffled collars and pointed hats. Whether riding on a unicycle, lying on a bed of nails, eating fire, juggling and tumbling and yes, even hitting each other over the head with a rubber chicken, it all was so entertaining for me and a contrast to the animal and super-human performances.

Carnivals also came to town in the summertime. There, we children took rides in the bumper cars, rollercoaster, carousel and Ferris wheel. For me, the bumper cars were the most fun, as we drove around the track and crashed into each other. It was also fun observing the various games of skill and games of chance. I specifically liked watching the operator at the roulette wheel as he attracted his audience through his loudspeaker, calling out to them, "Place your bets now, where you like or where you fancy, as the wee ball rolls, while she's rolling, while she's polling and where she stops nobody knows." His voice competed with the music of the carnival coming from the speakers mounted on the pole above, engulfing the whole town in sound. The carnival was a child's delight, with its games and food concessions of ice cream, sodas and treats that we never had at home.

Ballina also held an annual agricultural show each autumn, where farmers displayed their machinery, livestock and agricultural products for prizes. In the same manner, women presented their poultry, baked goods, jams, flower arrangements and handcrafts for awards. I attended the show with family members during my youth where we encountered neighbours and friends viewing the displays and activities. Of those, I found the show jumping most interesting to watch. It took the form of a steeple chase where horses jump over numerous and diverse fixed fence obstacles.[24] At the Ballina show, the

---

[24] The steeplechase originated in Ireland in the 18th century as thoroughbred horses raced from church steeple to church steeple across the country in contest. The tradition continues as a sporting activity today.

horses traversed the field in turn as their riders, dressed in black jackets and jodhpurs, competed. Judges sat in the grandstand broadcasting the flaws over their loudspeakers. This event attracted the largest number of viewers, partly due to its live performance and Ireland's enthusiasm for equestrian sports. For children, however, the rides on the Connemara or Shetland ponies, together with the great dog show, were the highlights that ensured a fun time for all.

In addition, the town sponsored an annual regatta, held at the Quay on the River Moy. The Quay, known as 'Mayo's last Discovery Point on the Wild Atlantic Way' offers a scenic location with a charming village.[25] Attending the festivities with Mam and Francie, we observed a variety of water contests, including sailing, canoeing, swimming and duck racing. The concept of duck-racing was new to me, and I wanted to participate. This would entail adopting a duck in my name for a price, and then throwing it into the river to compete against many other duck participants. From the bank, I could follow the race and anxiously watch for my duck to cross the finish line downstream, as the winner of the prize. Then, I would gladly return the duck to its rightful owner and donate the prize money to charity. Since my wish was not realised at the regatta, I thought about our ducks at home. They were then raised and independent from their mother hen. Perhaps I could train them to race and compete on our pond. Their mother hen might even show up on the bank to cheer them on. This time she would flap her wings in support rather than in fear, as she did when they were little.

Along with the water sports, the Ballina Regatta offered many other attractions such as the boat show and the arts and crafts exhibitions. Mingling through the crowds were vendors promoting their goods from wooden boxes strapped around their shoulders. The boxes contained apples, oranges, bananas, and sweets. For children, these treats were special but for adults, the homemade confectionaries, and fresh salmon sandwiches, all cooked and

---

[25] *The Wild Atlantic Way* is a tourist trail that stretches along Ireland's western seaboard. Covering more than 2,500 km in length, it is believed to be the world's longest tourist route. The journey is also known for its breathtaking beauty, offering spectacular scenery along the way.

prepared by the village women themselves, had greater appeal. In general, the regatta brought much excitement to this peaceful setting, reinforced by music from the band, as it sailed around on a boat in the lapping waters of the Moy River to the tune of:

> *"Cruising down the river on a Sunday afternoon*
> *With one you love, the sun above waiting for the moon*
> *The old accordion playing a sentimental tune*
> *Cruising down the river on a Sunday afternoon...."*

*Cruising Down the River* by Eily Beadell and Nell Tollerton (1946)

Part Six

# Religion

# 18

# Holy Ireland

Belief in God and the Church were hugely important aspects of life in the Ireland in which I grew up. The Catholic population continued the tradition of worship within a structure of parishes and dioceses, with bishops and priests presiding over them. In the diocese of Killala, which includes the town of Ballina, the bishop resided in his palace, together with servants, including a chauffeur to drive his car. Similarly, the parish priests lived comfortably with individual houses, servants, and automobiles. They all were supported by the local parishioners through periodic collections, resulting in a standard of living far superior to that of the farming community that they served. Seldom did the clergy socialise with the rural people. Instead, they could be seen playing golf and enjoying social activities with the established merchants and other town notables.

Within the Church itself, a class structure evolved over time. While the bankers and the merchants entered the cathedral via the tower or main door, the farmers and others found comfort entering through the penny or the half-penny doors located on both sides of the church. Though not mandatory, the standard donation at the main door was a shilling, which was significantly more than the penny and half-penny donations at the side doors. Attending Mass in the tower entrance was comparable to being at a fashion show. It was a place to be seen wearing one's best. It was where the ladies flaunted their style and furs, complete with a fox wrap around the shoulder. This was in sharp contrast to certain scenes at the side doors. Some of those attendees, especially country men, chose to remain at the entrance, kneeling on one knee, cap off, rosary beads in hand and cigarette dangling from the lips.

Attending Mass was a strict requirement for Sundays and Holy Days. As the church bell rang out, parishioners rushed to get there on time before the service began. Many travelled for miles by foot or by bike from the countryside. For women cyclists, the rush to get to church on time resembled a burlesque performance, with skirts flying high, offering a full display of petticoats, accentuated by increased pedalling. This always struck me as an amusing prelude to the Mass service which followed.

# 19

# Children and God

For Irish Catholic children, religious education was taught in the primary school system where we were told that our faith was the one true faith. We studied the catechism in preparation for the sacraments. At the age of seven, children celebrated their first Confession, the sacrament of Penance, followed by their first Holy Communion, the sacrament of the Eucharist. Children also learned religious hymns at primary school for the church choir. For rural children, the distance to church was considerable. Nevertheless, they walked there regardless of weather conditions.

Participating at their nine o'clock morning Mass on Sundays and Holy Days meant an early morning rise, and fasting from midnight was mandatory in order to receive Holy Communion. Once in church, the children fulfilled their duty to God with prayer and song for the one-hour service, enduring the long fast and the round-trip hike. I recall passing houses as I walked to and from Mass and feeling the pangs of hunger, accentuated by the aroma of cooking coming from various kitchens. This, I believed, was punishment for my sins, and I had better beat it to confession before finding myself in Hell with the Devil himself.

Monthly confession was a requirement for cleansing one's soul of sin. My list of sins grew longer each month, covering nonsense transgressions such as pulling a classmate's hair at school or stealing fists- full of sugar from Mam's cupboard. Standing in line outside the confession box, I would nervously review my litany. Then, once inside the dark confessionary, I wondered at times if the priest was there or if he had bolted, having spotted me in the queue as that child with the peculiar litany of sins. Relieved when the window slid open and the priest was there, I would bless myself and recite my list while hoping that the priest would go light on the penance. Over time, my penance for sins increased, with the priest telling me that I had better behave myself, since there was no end in sight to the increasing penance. Leaving the church, I always felt pure and cleansed and full of God's mercy.

It was routine for young girls to wear a white dress and veil for their first Communion, but not all families could afford such attire. For many families, the money was better spent on practical clothes and shoes for greater use, and reuse by younger siblings. There were no charity shops available to donate clothing so that all children could be equally dressed. The white outfits also were worn at the May procession celebrating the feast of the Virgin Mary. Led by the clergy carrying religious banners, the procession of participants marched along the streets next to the cathedral, while praying and singing in unison, *"Mary We Crown Thee with Blossoms, Queen of the Angels, Queen of the May…"* The little girls in white walked in front of the Virgin's statue carrying baskets of flowers, from which the petals were strewn along the streets and into the church yard. All other children, together with the general public, marched behind. It was a beautiful sight and festival, even for those little girls whose families could not afford the white outfit.

The Catholic faith and Church ceremonies were enriching for me as a child. In my home town of Ballina, in the diocese of Killala, I witnessed in 1950 the events leading to the consecration of our new bishop, Patrick O'Boyle, following the death of his predecessor, Bishop Naughton. It was a gala occasion. The entire town was aglow in celebration, featuring lights and sacred objects on buildings and homes. On the actual day of the consecration, I attended and observed the preparation and ceremony, with assistant bishops and attendants in their robes and vestments. Another memorable religious experience for me as a child was the Holy Week services, celebrated by observing the liturgical tradition of Tenebrae. This included a series of readings and psalms, chanted and recited by the clergy around the altar. The Tenebrae services marked the end of the Lenten season, leading up to Easter. It also signalled the end of my seven-week fast from sweets, as we were expected to abstain from a choice treat in honour of Lent. For me, the time had arrived to enjoy and indulge in my collected assortment, or share them with pals at our Easter picnic.

In my time, the Catholic Church had not yet come under scrutiny. The priests' sex scandals were unknown to the public at large. We were in the dark with limited or no media coverage and were largely controlled by the Church and the State. The victims, usually young boys, were afraid to speak out knowing that their parents and teachers would not have believed them since the clergy were then revered as Gods on Earth. We are better off today for knowing the truth and for having the confidence and education to challenge the misdeeds of our society.

# 20

# Pilgrimage to Croagh Patrick

While there are many well-known pilgrimage sites in Ireland such as Knock, Lough Derg and *Gleann Cholm Cille* among others, where the faithful seek penance, Croagh Patrick is the most famous. Known locally as *The Reek,* meaning a stack, Croagh Patrick is considered Ireland's holiest mountain. With a steep elevation of 2,500 feet, it has proven to be a difficult climb to reach the small summit chapel for atonement. According to legend, it is where Saint Patrick fasted for forty days in the year 441.

> *"There's a dear little plant that grows in our Isle.*
> *'Twas Saint Patrick himself sure that set it*
> *And the sun on his labour with pleasure did smile*
> *And with dew from his eye often wet it…"*

*The Dear Little Shamrock* by Andrew Cherry (1762-1812)

Situated in County Mayo, local Catholics were expected to join the thousands of pilgrims on the last weekend of July to honour the saint.

Setting off in a van, a group of us, male and female teenagers, headed for *The Reek* on one typically wet Saturday evening. Arriving at the base, we braced ourselves for the muddy hike, wearing inadequate boots and clothing. We each carried an ash plant for a walking stick as we climbed to the summit, slipping and sliding in the mud all the way.

For the final stretch of the climb, I was helped along by my neighbour, Vivian Loftus, who held my arm, preventing me from sliding backwards and falling. Without his strength, I could not have reached the top. After attending Mass and receiving Holy Communion in the wee chapel at the top, we prepared to descend. As the rains continued to fall, our descent became infinitely more difficult, with the loose gravel giving way beneath our feet and visibility becoming poorer. Along the way, we met lots of neighbours and friends either climbing or descending. For many, this was a night of fun, beginning with a visit to the pub. Consequently, many pilgrims were well *oiled* as they climbed. But for most, it was a religious pilgrimage to atone for sin. Some even choose to climb the mountain barefoot, as an act of penance.[26]

Preparing for our descent

---

[26] Many tourists to Ireland visit Croagh Patrick because it is connected to their family history. One of the most notable was Grace Kelly, whose ancestors came from the adjacent town of Westport. Grace climbed a portion of the mountain, together with an entourage of security and press. Following her visit, the whole of Ireland with Kelly as a family name made claim to their American cousin.

# 21

# The Stations

The mission came to our town every October, dedicating one week each for men, women, and children. Outside the cathedral, stalls were set up to sell religious objects that were blessed by the missioners. It was the custom to have the missioners celebrate Mass in a village home. Such hosting was known as the Stations. This tradition dates back to the Penal Laws of the 16th century when it was forbidden for Catholic priests to hold Mass in public. As an alternative, the service was performed secretly in private homes. Although the penal laws eventually passed into history in the 1700s, the response to these laws continued. Selected by the Church, families took turns hosting the Stations. While it was a great honour to be chosen, it also was a great expense for a family, as it meant preparing the entire house, both inside and out. Painting, repairing, decorating, and cooking were necessary without reimbursement from the Church or the community. Since most village houses were three-room cottages, it was necessary to reserve one room for hearing confessions and a second for serving breakfast. This left the kitchen for holding the Mass with the kitchen table as a makeshift altar. Gathered around the room, villagers participated in the service and received Holy Communion. During the Mass donations were collected for the priests' fund. It was best to give generously and avoid embarrassment since individual contributions were at times publicly announced from the church pulpit, "Gráinne Kelly, nothing." Such a practice by the Church was normal then as a way to humiliate those who gave less than expected or in some cases gave nothing, depending on the worshipers' means at that time. Following the Mass at the Stations, breakfast was served, first to the priests, using the hosts finest linens and table settings. The Station service ended once the priests departed. It was then time for gaiety with invitations extended to neighbouring villagers, family members and friends. Very often, the merriment continued into the night, with music, song and dance, and with food and drink galore.

*"With a toot on the flute and the twiddle on the fiddle-o!*
*Hopping in the middle, like a herrin' on the griddle-o!*
*Up! down, hands around crossing to the wall-o!*
*Hadn't we the gaiety at Phil the Fluter's ball…"*

*Phil The Fluter's Ball* by William Percy French (1854-1920)

Although our house was chosen to host the Stations during my youth, I was unable to participate due to school obligations. I did, however, attend a few held in neighbouring houses. Joining in the Mass and receiving the sacraments in a village home, surrounded by neighbours, was a moving experience for me. It was also interesting to meet the missioners, who came from various regions of Ireland. Mam was in much demand in assisting neighbours with the decorating and the serving of the priests' breakfast. One villager, named Ambrose, sought her help when it came to his turn to host the Stations. Taking full charge, Mam got his house in order and represented him as the hostess for the occasion.

Ambrose, a bachelor farmer, lived in a three-bedroomed house with a slated roof. This tall, slender man walked with a slight limp, keeping his head down and rarely spoke to anyone. He blamed a neighbouring woman, named Brid, unjustly for everything and anything missing around his house, including cabbages and apples from his garden. Ambrose liked to hang out at night-time next to the Downhill Hotel, peeping around a telegraph pole, to watch the hotel girls rotate their shifts at the hotel. His odd behaviour proved to be harmless in all cases, qualifying him as yet another village character.

# 22

# Christmas Festivities

In rural Ireland of the 1950s, the Christmas season was more religious than commercial. We visited the nativity crib at the cathedral and attended midnight Mass on Christmas Eve. Preparations began weeks in advance, starting with the making of Christmas cakes and puddings. For such, we shopped in town for dried fruits, spices and other necessary ingredients. The cakes were varied, including porter cakes made with Guinness stout as an alternative ingredient to whiskey or sherry. Following the baking process, all fruit cakes were secured in airtight tins and, like a good wine, tasted better with age. In making the plum pudding, the ingredients were tied in a muslin cloth and steamed for several hours. When cooked, the pudding was hung from the kitchen ceiling for days to allow it to set and then later placed on the table with a sprig of holly in its centre. Presented as dessert, this classic holiday pudding was often taken to the dining area in flames and served heated with hot rum sauce. These traditional fruit cakes and puddings were speciality dishes for the Irish Christmas feast.

In Ballina, shopkeepers distributed food hampers and Christmas boxes to loyal customers in appreciation of their business during the year. Pubs were busy as friends treated each other to a Christmas drink, especially after having met by chance in town. *"Musha,* is it yourself that's in it?" was a common greeting. For a second encounter on the same day, the greeting might be, "Well, have *ya* not gone home yet?" as they stood for a time recapping the day's events. Many of the visitors in town were home on holidays from their jobs elsewhere, adding to the spirit of the season. Turkeys, geese, and other fowl were traded on the open market. Money from the sale of the birds allowed for, 'Bringing home the Christmas,' consisting of food and drink and household needs.[27] It was a delight to see such revelry, as the farmers returned from town with carts loaded with Christmas cheer.

> *"The holly green, the ivy green.*
> *The prettiest picture you've ever seen.*
> *It's Christmas in Killarney*
> *With all of the folks at home ... "*

*Christmas in Killarney* by John Redmond, James Cavanaugh,
Frank Weldon (1950)

For us children, the decorating of the home brought much joy, from the red-berried holly branches placed over the hanging pictures to the nativity scene, purchased with our spare pennies. In addition, we strung coloured paper chains across the ceilings, with blown-up balloons or paper fans in the centre. Few homes then had Christmas trees, since there were no tree farms to provide them. As a substitute, we used small bushes or treetops, which we placed on a stool for display. To decorate our tree, we used Christmas cards, cotton balls, tinsel icicles, and a few affordable ornaments. On the top, we

---

[27] In local villages during my time, liquor was not kept in the homes. At Christmas or for special occasions, the farmers brought home a bottle of whiskey, sherry or port to share with visitors. For those farmers who succeeded in completing their home brew, an extra celebration was called for.

placed a Fairy Godmother with stretched wings. As a young girl, I got the most pleasure from the Christmas tree. Shopping for ornaments in town was special. Inside the shop, I browsed for hours looking at the selection of delicate glass bulbs in varying colours and shapes. I also shopped for tiny candles and their little holders to clip onto the branches, but unlit to prevent fire. Keeping our dogs away from the tree became an issue, since they liked to stand next to it wagging their tails, and at times sent the decorations into orbit, with the odd glass ones smashing onto the floor.

As a final sample of the season, a blessed candle stood inside on the kitchen windowsill ready to be lit on Christmas Eve.

Pappy, the post man, delivered the mail and parcels on his bike. Starting early in the morning, he first went to the post office in Ballina to pick up his daily deliveries. Then, he biked all day, covering a large territory of villages. With no van service for packages, Pappy's bike was equipped to hold them. The packages varied from parcels of clothing from abroad to turkeys ready to cook during the holiday season. For letters, he carried a large canvas sack across his shoulder, with a flap to cover the contents. Dressed in his postal uniform complete with cap, gloves and cape, Pappy completed his rounds. During the winter months his job was especially difficult, due to weather conditions. Yet, snow, sleet, frost, ice, rain and wind did not deter Pappy. Over time, he got to

know all the villagers by name. Approaching our house, he would call out, "Maggie!" Hearing his call, Mam rushed to greet him at our gate, where they chatted for some time. Pappy was always invited in for tea and cake. At Christmas time, the treat became a glass of whiskey. Consequently, Pappy was well *oiled* from the many treats he received during the holiday season. Somehow, he got his job done free of accidents. Mail for our house was usually light throughout the year. It increased at Christmas time with letters, cards and parcels from abroad. Consequently, I looked forward to Pappy's call at *Nollag*, meaning Christmas in Irish, in the hopes of receiving parcels and cards from America or England. Relatives in America were sure to enclose a few dollars with their cards, together with photographs of family members dressed in Christmas colours next to a glowing fire. Thus, giving us the impression that they were all so comfortable. The parcels from America contained unfamiliar stuff such as candy canes, chewing gum and bubble gum, convincing us that the *Gods must be Crazy* to have come up with such peculiar stuff.

A special visitor to our house at Christmas was Charley Ferguson, who dropped by to collect the priests' dues.[28] In the process, he shared a drink of whiskey with Mam. Charlie was a pillar in the community. He lived in our village with his wife Mary and their lovely family. Theirs was a friendly house with children of all ages for playmates and pals. Growing up, I always associated Charlie with Christmas and the joys of the season.

In addition to celebrating the holidays with Pappy and Charlie, it was customary for neighbours, friends, and relatives to visit each other. Without automobiles, they either walked or biked on the dark roads, bracing themselves for the weather. Usually, it was frosty and cold, but they were undeterred. As a young girl, I eagerly listened for our gate to rattle in anticipation of Christmas visitors. For those that came, our two dogs greeted them first, with their barks of welcome. Then, the latch lifted on our front door, and the visitors stepped right in. The conversation lasted for hours, as the Christmas food was served together with a few glasses of whiskey, sherry,

---

[28] Charlie was our village volunteer for the Church collections. He remained in this role during my childhood years. The Christmas collection was major, covering all villages and towns in the parish. The collected proceeds helped support the Church and the clergy of the parish.

or port. In turn, Mam also went visiting, taking her two daughters with her. We walked the round-trip distances at night-time, with Mam holding our hands. Along the way, we observed millions of stars in the sky above, sparkling brightly through the clear unpolluted atmosphere. In their midst, we noted some falling stars, which we believed were souls on their way to Heaven. We also gazed at the moon, trying to make out the features of the 'man in the moon.' Occasionally, we were blessed with a full moon that illuminated our surroundings and provided us with light for our journey. Arriving at our destination, our hosts welcomed us warmly, offering their holiday treats. As the adults chatted away, we children focused on the Christmas tree ornaments and the toys, usually dolls and their regalia. I enjoyed comparing the decorations and the Christmas trees with ours at home, but when it came to the fancy dolls and sophisticated toys, there was little of ours to compare. For me, however, that brand-new coper penny that Mam gave each of her children, placing it in the palm of our hands *each Nollag* to bring us good luck for the coming year, was the most precious gift of all. In general, Christmas was a joyous season of peace and spirituality, prompting generosity and goodwill throughout the villages and the community.

.

Part Seven

# Education

# 23

# Schools and Schooling

The levels of education in Ireland are primary school, secondary school, and university, with primary at all times compulsory and free. In recent decades, significant progress has been made in the Irish educational system, starting in the mid-1960s with the introduction of free post-primary education. Before then, only a fraction of Irish youth went on to receive a second-level education. The rest were leaving full-time schooling at the tender age of thirteen or fourteen, once they completed the primary certificate. This meant that only the well-off families could afford to send their children to secondary school. Few scholarships were granted.

For the children of lesser means who qualified, there still remained the issue of money for books, clothing and lodging. Some of those who accepted scholarships ended up dropping out from embarrassment or teasing from their better-off classmates. Furthermore, discrimination sometimes took place in the granting of scholarships based on needs in the country, such as a shortage of Protestant teachers in rural districts. From time-to-time, a teacher would recognise a child's potential and offer to finance his or her second-level education, but the family might decline due to the child's commitment to the farm and the need to support younger siblings. Great intelligence was wasted under this educational system as many fine young minds were neglected. It was not uncommon to find the brighter but less privileged pupils assisting the more privileged ones with homework and lessons. Yet, the latter progressed into higher education and the professions, while the former went to work on the farms or in the trades.

In my time, the primary or national schools were thinly dispersed throughout the countryside, often serving many surrounding villages. Apart from the odd private school, primary schools were public and Catholic. The teachers were a mixture of lay men and women, nuns, and priests, with the Catholic Church overseeing the schools. Prayers and Catholic teachings were part of the curriculum. For the non-Catholic students, they received their own religious teachings at their churches. The education at the primary level was of high standard with a diverse curriculum. In addition to the required reading, writing and arithmetic, much emphasis was given to literature, poetry, history, and geography. Many subjects were taught in Irish, with the objective of replacing English with Irish as the national spoken language. Fluency in Irish was a criterion for college entrance leading to high-level jobs, particularly those in government.

With no special needs education, all children attended their local national school regardless of abilities, and some suffered greatly as a result. Caning as punishment was permitted at the national school level with no rules established for its use.[29] This practice was not monitored by authorities. It was applied at the teacher's discretion for poor learning or for bad behaviour. Teachers might also hold grudges against certain families for various reasons. For instance, in certain cases teachers owned and operated farms in the local villages. As issues arose with adjacent landowners, the children from such

---

[29] Caning is a form of physical punishment, using a cane or a rod, and applied as slaps on the bare palms of the hands. The slaps left painful red marks or blisters that could last for some time.

farms might be mistreated at the hands of the teacher. While none of us pupils escaped an odd slap from time-to-time, many others were not so fortunate. Believing that they had learning disabilities, their true talents untapped, they stood frozen in fear from frequent teacher canings in the classroom, and in front of fellow classmates until 1982 when it was deemed a criminal offence to hit a student.

# 24

# Primary Schooling

For my primary education, I attended Behy school. *Behy* is the Irish word for birch land, although many other tree species grew on the school's grounds. Located about three miles from the town of Ballina, the school dates back to 1878, thirty years after the Irish famine. Initially it was a one-room schoolhouse with only one teacher, Mr. John Keating. By 1944 it had expanded to four rooms and four teachers, and remained as such for the

duration of my schooling there. The building consisted of two large rooms with a sliding partition in the centre of each, thus creating four separate classrooms. The sliding partitions allowed for flexibility in hosting events. Upon entering the school, one stepped into a large hallway where pupils hung their coats and congregated. There was no indoor plumbing or running water. Dry toilets stood on the grounds outside, but in general sanitation was minimal.

Attending Behy school was a memorable experience, as we students walked there through the bogs and dirt roads, braving the weather conditions. Leaving home at nine o'clock in the morning and returning in the afternoon at four, we carried our lunches in our school bags, consisting of little more than two slices of bread with butter in between and a small bottle of milk to drink. The school rooms were unheated, which meant that in bad weather we sat at our desks in damp or wet clothes and shoes throughout the day. While each classroom had a fireplace at one end where the teachers sat, the heat did not disperse throughout the room. It was expected that local farmers provide the fuel or turf to heat the school. While some did deliver cart loads of turf, others did not, resulting in a shortfall. To cover the deficit, children were asked to carry two sods of turf in their arms to school on class days during the winter months.

This was an inadequate and unsuccessful solution to our shivers, coughs, and sniffles. Home remedies were the answer to cure our ailments, with Vicks medicines, cod-liver oil, and flannel vests. For wounds, there was the all-purposeful bottle of iodine that stung sharply when applied, together with the hot poultice of white bread to treat infections. Doctors' care was unheard of for us children except for vaccinations received at school for such diseases as smallpox, diphtheria, and polio, some of which left permanent pock marks on our arms. Dentists also showed up at school periodically to treat children's cavities, rewarded with two days leave from class. The time off was the appeal for me as I lined up with an imaginary tooth ache. Arriving home minus one perfect tooth a *bleddy* numb jaw, Mam was surprised knowing that my teeth were all fine but that she dared not question the authorities. It appeared that pulling teeth was the dentists' specialty in rural Ireland then, predating orthodontists and other dental care for children's teeth. The saddest day off at Behy school was for the death of Maureen Gallagher, whose parents taught at the school, and who died as a teenager from tuberculosis (TB). This disease was spreading rapidly around our country then with deaths mounting and buildings being converted into sanitoriums in every town.[30] While many of those make-shift hospitals have since been refurbished into modern facilities, I continue to associate them with this horrible disease.

The educational system at Behy school was rigid. We began our day by greeting our teachers in Irish as we waited for the doors to open. Next, we lined up to buy our school supplies from the master but only succeeded if our request in Irish was perfect. Likewise, permission to go to the toilet was a challenge, as we raised our hands requesting leave in Irish. By the time permission was granted, the urge had often passed. Much emphasis was given to discipline and respect for authority. Pupils did not question or dispute the teachings and they stood with respect as superiors entered and left the classroom. Our master, Hugh Gallagher, had a forty-year tenure at Behy school. His wife, Eileen, also taught there where, together with fellow teachers, they educated their six children as part of the student body. Their daughter named Philo was my age and we progressed together from grade to grade in our classroom with fellow pupils. Petite with long, thick, curly hair, Philo demonstrated her status as the teachers' daughter with confidence in the classroom. Her father was indeed a brilliant man with high ratings for teaching. He attracted students to his school from areas outside of his district, and even from Ballina town. Among those were the Reilly children who walked the three-mile distance, carrying their books and lunch in their school bags. In addition, they were tasked with carrying a large can of fresh drinking

---

[30] Ciara Breathnach writing for *The Irish Times* on March 23rd, 2020, comments, "At a time when other European countries had seen a mortality decline after the Second World War, Ireland was still in the grip of a tuberculosis epidemic."

water from the Bunree well for the teachers use only. Other more affluent children cycled the journey from Ballina. In my class alone, I recall several such commuters, Brendan, Colm, Danny, John and Liam among others. They were sent by their prosperous families to receive a good education in preparation for college followed by professional jobs. They had company in transit, since their teachers, excluding the Gallaghers in their automobile, also cycled from Ballina to their posts at Behy school.

Lunch time offered a chance to eat our sandwiches and join in play with fellow pupils. This one-hour period was the only scheduled break in the school day. Boys and girls played separately in their own space, with boys engaged in Gaelic football and soccer, while the girls joined hands in playing ring-around-the-rosy. This was one of my favourite games as I recall holding the hand of one girl with a physical condition and pulling her along in play with the rest of us. One of our leaders in sporting activities was a classmate named Rita, a tall pretty girl who wore her blonde hair in ringlets. She and I were born four days apart and our parents liked to compare our developments.

Rita, together with her brother Bobby, were among the few non-Catholic children attending Behy school then. Since they did not participate in the school's religious education, they enjoyed an extra lunch hour. As the bell rang signalling the end of lunchtime, certain kids rushed to their classrooms in the hope of reaching there first to grab the left-over food from our teachers' lunch. Those children were hungry and, in some cases, malnourished. Dinner was awaiting them once they reached home, as was work, since most had chores to perform on the family farms, leaving little time for marble pitching on the road home.

Aware of his established reputation as a good teacher, Mr. Gallagher set high standards for his students, with little tolerance for 'slow learning.' Consequently, many pupils were mistreated by him, resulting in much resentment and anger. He had his favourite families, and treated those children accordingly. Lucky for me, I was among the chosen ones. He respected my brother Jim and my cousin, Mary Connor, for their intelligence as pupils at Behy school, and expected the same of other family members. "*Tusa Mairead*" (you Margaret) he would say in a soft voice after going around the class seeking the answer to his question, believing that I would have it. He demonstrated a fondness for my family in many ways, especially for his farming needs. At springtime, he would order a few bags of potato sprouts from Mam to plant in his garden. Sending the order through me, he would pin a pound note on my cardigan to take home as payment. Mam, together with my two brothers, would then pick the very best potato sprouts and deliver them to the master's house. Generations of my family have passed through Behy school, both before and after my education there. Browsing through the school's roll books in search of family members, it is comforting to spot their names, and to know that this continuity is maintained.

Steps were taken to upgrade and maintain the Behy school facilities in my time. Tickets were sold and raffles held to raise money for improvements. Pupils were given books of tickets to sell in their neighbourhoods. For us children, this was a labour of love in support of our school since no rewards were offered for our efforts or for our results. I recall going from house to house in the local villages promoting the cause, and then turning over the proceeds together with the ticket stubs. High on the list for improvements were to paint the school's interior and exterior and to replace the outdoor lavatories with flush toilets. While subscribers understood the need to paint the school for maintenance purposes, they reacted strongly to the concept of flush toilets. They could be heard complaining, "What do they need flush toilets for? A lot of flush toilets we had in our day at school. How will flush toilets help the children with their lessons?" Nevertheless, a school concert was organised to attract funding. Much planning was necessary to prepare children for their various roles, covering song, poetry, readings and theatrical performances. Past pupils were invited to share their talents. The opening song of the evening was *A Nation Once Again* sung by my brother John with his gifted baritone voice. This was followed by other traditional ballads such as *Wrap the Green Flag Around Me*, *The Minstrel Boy*, and many others, sung by adept pupils. But the song that was special for me was *Bonnie Mary of Argyle* sung by my sister Francie. The agenda for the evening included a variety of solo, duet and group performances, in both Irish and in English. A fun time was had by all, resulting in praise for the teachers and performers, and money *galore* for the much-needed painting and flush toilets poured in.

Its curriculum has been diversified considerably to include athletics for both boys and girls, with many resulting champions. During my time, sporting games, like Gaelic football and soccer, were for boys only.[31]

---

[31] Father Peter Quinn, past pupil of Behy school and former footballer for the Mayo team, presenting his trophy ball to young pupils at the school.

Looking back, I have fond memories of Behy school. I left there with a solid foundation in the 3R's, together with a strong introduction to world history and geography. I also left there knowing a selection of Gregorian chants in Latin, taught to my class for a church performance by my favourite teacher, Mrs. Bridge Mulderrig. I take pride in singing the sacred songs at church services while friends wonder where I learned them.

At Behy school, I made childhood friendships that have endured. My closest pal was Kitty Ruddy.[32] As neighbours, we shared the walk back and forth to school, sat next to each other in the classroom and even ate our individual lunches privately together. Kitty was a pretty girl with big brown eyes and long blonde hair that she oftentimes wore in braids around her head. She was devoted to her two younger brothers, Edward and Paddy, and was tasked with introducing Edward to Behy school. With much resistance on his part, Kitty and I dragged the boy, as he kicked and screamed, along the bog road to his infant class. After school hours, Kitty and I did our homework together and also found time for play. The games we especially liked were skip rope and joint steps, for which we assigned ungrateful roles to Edward and Paddy, before turning in for a new day of schooling.

---

[32] Kitty's aunt, Miss Claire Ruddy, established and operated a private primary school in Ballina where she taught children from local affluent families. Among them was Mary Robinson, Ireland's first female president.

# 25

# Vocational Schooling

Vocational or technical schools in Ireland expanded during the 1950s in order to educate and develop its youth for the job market. The schools were governed by Vocational Educational Committees (VECs) to ensure that the subjects offered were both practical and academic. This two-year schooling programme was affordable for the average family to teach their children marketable employment skills. For boys, the emphasis was on carpentry and mechanics, while for girls it was on home economics and secretarial studies. Such schools could be found in major towns across the country.

The Ballina Vocational School, *The Tech*, was inaugurated by the Mayo VEC following the introduction of the Vocational Educational Act of the 1930s. In my time, *The Tech* was centrally located next to the Ballina Cathedral. Its facility was modern and spacious, with up to ten classrooms. Certain classrooms were dedicated to gender studies, including the kitchen, which was exclusive for female cooking and sewing classes. The teachers were specialists in their individual disciplines. Apart from the few co-ed subjects offered, women taught female related courses while men taught male related classes. In accordance with VEC standards, the Ballina Tech emphasised practical studies geared towards preparing its students for employment.

My two years at the Ballina Tech broadened my horizons. The school attracted students from the surrounding districts as well as from the town. To the town kids, we country folk were known as *Culchies* lacking in sophistication and elegance, with hayseeds in our ears and cobwebs in our hair. Arriving on our bikes, we resembled a swarm of locusts invading their territory. One classmate, named Freda, liked to joke and, at times, mimic our brogues. Freda, tall and slender with her long hair tied in a ponytail, was a lot of fun in the classroom. In turn, we *Culchies* referred to town kids as *Town Slickers,* lacking a proper appreciation of nature, as the poem we learned at school put it:

> *"God help the boy who never sees*
> *The butterflies, the birds, the bees*
> *Not hears the music of the breeze*
> *When zephyrs soft are blowing…"*

*God Help the Boy* by Nixon D. Waterman (1859-1944)

So began my Tech experience.

As expected, the majority of the subjects were gender related, with boys and girls studying separately. The woodwork, metalwork, design and drawing classes for boys led them to apprenticeship programmes with established firms in the town and beyond. Similarly, the commerce, business methods and domestic science classes for girls prepared them for secretarial and business roles. In preparation for our commerce studies, we were required to purchase supplies of journals, ledgers and bottles of red and black inks. While briefcases were recommended to carry our books and supplies, not all of us could afford such luxury. I observed certain classmates, Loretta and Bea, with their school materials neatly arranged in their brand-new briefcases and was impressed with the layout for securing the contents. Most of us, however, continued to use our school bags knowing that our inks were subject to spill, especially since many of us commuted by bike. Consequently, my bookkeeping numbers ended up in the red, as the red ink leaked out. This could have been a true introduction for many local businesses, as they struggled to turn red to black in creative ways.

For our typing class, we received instructions on the importance of posture and positioning, as we sat facing the typewriters. Looking down at the keyboard was forbidden since the assignments were written on the blackboard behind the teacher. Staring straight ahead, fingers on keys and backs stiffened, we quickly learned that the typewriters were equally stiff, as we moved the levers back and forth. Our grades were based on accuracy and speed in completing the assignment within a given timeframe set by a timer. The resulting noise generated from a room full of typewriters, with the clicking and clacking of keys, together with the ringing of bells from each carriage return, would have scared the devil from his den. Few errors were allowed to pass the test, which in most cases meant re-typing the entire assignment over from start. Alas, if only word processing had been invented sooner, how easier our lives would have been.

As part of our business education, we also studied Gregg shorthand. Invented by John Robert Gregg in the late 1800s, this popular form of pen stenography was based on elliptical figures and lines. At *The Tech* we used the simplified version, published in 1949. This reduced form, allowed for a maximum speed of 150 words per minute (WPM), with a norm of 100 to 120 WPM for business stenography. Speed and accuracy were the criteria for grading at *The Tech* to qualify students for secretarial jobs in business. One classmate in particular, named Eileen, enjoyed a successful career in the British Isles as a secretary by applying her Tech schooling. Today in her retirement, she continues to use her skills as a volunteer for the Senior Citizen Club of Ballina, her home-town.

Moving into the domestic science classes was a welcome relief from the commerce studies. Most enjoyable were the cooking courses that culminated in the making of our individual Christmas cakes. These cakes contained certain elements of a standard fruit cake for which students were obligated to provide the necessary ingredients. Once the cakes were baked, we learned to decorate them with finishing touches for presentation. We started with marzipan as a first layer which we made from crushed almonds. This was then topped with royal icing that, once hardened, allowed for creative decorating. The themes were numerous, centred on winter and holiday scenes, and the end result represented works of culinary art. However, getting our prizes home intact on our bikes became an issue. We first sealed our precious cakes in airtight tins and then double secured them in thick cardboard boxes that fastened snugly onto the carriers of our bikes. Taking off with our cargo, my friend Noreen and I pedalled along on the icy road towards home.[33] Rounding a corner, our bikes collided into each other. As we struggled to stand up, we watched our cakes slide ahead into the slush. Not knowing what to expect, we rescued the airtight tins from the disintegrated cardboard boxes. Then, nervously peeling open the lids, we were elated to see our treasured cakes in perfect order to present to our families as our special gift for the holidays.

The school's kitchen stove was used for our cooking classes. It was the students' responsibility to maintain its coal fire for cooking. One day, our teacher, an attractive slender lady wearing a spotless white uniform, sent me, together with another classmate, to the caretaker's furnace for additional coal. To get there, it was necessary to go outside, since the furnace was located in a separate building behind the school. When we arrived, the caretaker filled a metal basin with live coals, and sent us on our way. Holding the rim of the basin with our bare hands, we moved quickly to reach the kitchen. As the heat from the coals reached the rim, we were forced to drop the basin onto the

---

[33] Noreen and I have been lifetime friends. Raised in adjacent villages, we first met at the age of three while visiting her house with my father. Our friendship grew as teenagers, attending the same schools and social gatherings. For some years, we went our separate ways, she to London for a nursing career and me to the U.S. for a career in business. In recent years, we have reconnected and find that our relationship is stronger than ever as we remines about our youth and share our common interests. Noreen, petite and cute with her big blue eyes and warm smile, is a very special lady with a most positive disposition.

floor. By then we were inside the school, which had a linoleum floor covering. Immediately, the floor started to burn, the smoke rose, and doors opened as people rushed to escape. There we stood, surrounded by the commotion. It can be truly said that we left our mark on *The Tech*.

Among the few co-ed courses offered was literature, bringing girls and boys together in the same classroom. This subject was taught by Mr. Nolan who was also the school's principal. A distinguished gentleman and erudite, his son, Colm, was among my classmates at Behy school. Mr. Nolan was my favourite teacher while at *The Tech*, partly due to his specialty in English literature and the classics. As his students, we covered a selection of Shakespeare's most popular sonnets. Reading aloud, with emphasis placed on certain syllables, we followed the rhythms of the poems. Next, we analysed the meaning behind the writings and how Shakespeare used nature and the seasons to symbolise beauty and time. Along with the sonnets, we studied a selection of Shakespeare's plays. In the classroom, we took turns reading aloud the soliloquies from *Hamlet*, including, *"To be or not to be…"* as the prince compared death to a little sleep. We also covered *Macbeth* and the soliloquy, *"Is this a dagger which I see before me…"* as Macbeth decided to kill the king and take over the crown for himself. When it came to Lady Macbeth's words of persuasion to murder Duncan, *"I have given suck and know how tender 'tis to love…"* silence befell the class followed by spurts of titters. By this time, we students were learning the facts of life from each other, never from a teacher or from a parent, and such references were a source of both embarrassment and amusement.

We enjoyed the social activities organised at *The Tech* for its students. The most popular was the annual outing to Mayo's historical and scenic spots, such as Clew Bay and Mulranny.[34] On such outings, we received lessons on

---

[34] Clew Bay, an ocean bay, has numerous islands, many of which are Ireland's best examples of limestone drumlins. One such island was owned by the former Beatle, John Lennon, as his peaceful hideaway. Clew Bay is nestled between Croagh Patrick and the Nephin mountain range. The islands offer picturesque little villages, including *Mulranny*, Irish for hill of ferns. Mulranny is known for its exotic plants of ferns and fuchsias. It is also known for its long sandy beach, and is a popular tourist destination. This was enhanced in recent years by its award as a "European Destination of Excellence" (EDEN).

the landscape, explored the surrounding beauty, competed for prizes in sporting events and picnicked by the waters. Packed into a chartered bus, we joined in song as we travelled the round trip. Next to the outings in popularity were the holiday concerts for Christmas and summer breaks. Selected by the teachers to perform based on talent, students prepared for their roles, be it song, poetry, or readings. For Christmas leave, the theme was on that season, with traditional holiday song and verse. The song that I most recall for its contrast at one concert was *"Santo Natale, Santo Natale, this is my way of saying Merry Christmas to you..."* sung by a fellow student named P.J. on whom I had my first teenage crush, blushing considerably each time he passed me by.

Attending school in the town exposed rural children to shopping and market activities. With some coppers to spend, we treated ourselves to ice cream and sweets. My friend Noreen and I liked to drop into Mary Melvin's tiny sweet shop, where we ordered a penny's worth of bulls' eyes, a round black candy ball with white stripes. Mary was an elderly lady who depended on her shop for her livelihood. Therefore, she did not really welcome our custom, given our miniscule shopping list. Standing behind the counter, Mary would mutter to herself upon hearing our tall order. Then, reluctantly, she turned her back to scoop up the sweets from a jar, filling two small brown paper bags for us, while we stood there making faces. Returning to the classroom, we kept our precious purchase to ourselves, realising that our sweets could not compare with the more expensive selections made by some of our classmates. In particular, a student named Teresa, was known for her rich assortments which she kept in her open schoolbag. Sitting in the row of seats behind her, I would start to salivate, like Pavlov's dogs, in anticipation of a treat. Teresa was generous about sharing her sweets with classmates in adjacent seats, which is why I subconsciously positioned myself behind her.

Our teachers at *The Tech* worked hard to prepare us for the world outside. Most had confidence in our abilities and futures. Our commerce teacher, however, thought otherwise. A stout woman, wearing dangling jewellery and gobs of red lipstick reaching her nose, she believed that we were all doomed. Standing at the top of the classroom behind her desk, hands clasped and eyes looking towards the heavens, she pray*ed,* "God help you poor lost souls going out into the big, wide, open world, without one word in your heads." While we may have been disruptive in the classroom, playing tricks on each other along the way, we all had great potential. Some of our classmates stayed local, finding work as secretaries, or entering apprenticeship programmes for additional training, but the majority of us left to find work elsewhere, or to pursue careers requiring specific training. Still others, following in the footsteps of so many Irish, emigrated to England or America for their jobs and their lives.

Part Eight

# Adolescence

# 26

# Dancing on the Bridge

We learned to dance on a local bridge situated in the village of Corrimbla, a distance of about four miles from the town of Ballina.

*"I'm thinking tonight of the old rustic bridge*
*That bends o'er the murmuring stream*
*It was there Maggie dear with our hearts full of cheer*
*We strayed 'neath the moon's gentle beam…"*

*The Old Rustic Bridge by The Mill* by Thomas Peter Keenan (1866-1927)

In the summer twilight, members of the Murray family brought along their accordion and played there into the late evening. This extraordinary family of twelve children lived on a farm next to the Corrimbla bridge. Many of them worked in England to help support their farm. Naturally talented, they brought their self-taught accordion music to the outdoors for all to enjoy. The sound of their music from the bridge could be heard for miles in the distance. Those of us who attended were either in our teens or early twenties.

Our parents objected to our participation, since many of us were still in school, and this was seen as a distraction. Parents also were concerned about us, "Wearing the soles and heels off your shoes." But our shoes already had many holes in the soles, so a few more made little difference. One neighbour woman, Mrs. Margaret Ann Melvin, complained about her son Tommy: "He's gone off to the bridge with a *swelled head of cheek*," meaning that he was all too full of himself. Nevertheless, we took off on our bikes, pretending that we were visiting friends. Placing my family's small white terrier dog, named Cookie, in the basket of my bike, I pedalled off to the next village to meet up with my friend Noreen. Together with the dog, we continued on to the bridge. Once there, I joined in the dancing while swinging Cookie around by his two front paws, as he moved on his hind legs, keeping step to the music.

With so many young bachelors attending, the females were considerably outnumbered. These young men, namely the McGowan brothers, the Melvin brothers and the Murray brothers among others, were all from local village farms, most of whom never married due to changing demographics. We took turns changing partners as we danced around and around under the stars. The dancing on the bridge, however, came to an abrupt end when the parish priests caught wind of it. Arriving unexpectedly one evening in their fancy car, they took note of our ages. Then, claiming that this activity kept school age children from their homework and lessons, the Church won out, and the dancing stopped. For all of us who participated, dancing on the bridge was fun while it lasted. There, we learned to waltz, foxtrot, quick-step, and swing.

One young lady, Kathleen Murray, who later won many prizes in America for her ballroom dancing, never forgot where it all began 'on the old rustic bridge near her home.'

# 27

# The Country Hall

For our first ballroom dance experience we cycled to Bonniconlon, a town about seven miles from home. To dress for the dance, my friend Noreen and I took the liberty of wearing the best outfits belonging to her older sister, Myra. For finishing touches, we helped ourselves to Myra's makeup, hairspray, and perfume. We were fortunate that Noreen's Mam adored watching the pair of us, enjoying our antics and mischievous behaviour, and always covered for us. Years later, when I visited Noreen's Mam during my first trip home from America, I was greeted with hugs and tears as the dear woman recalled those precious years gone by.

Arriving at Bonniconlon, we left our bikes along a ditch on a side road close to the dance hall. This was a rural country hall where local bands performed. The music was mostly traditional Irish rather than modern. Inside the hall, the men sat on one side and the women on the other. Once a dance number was announced by the band, the men slid across the floor to ask a lady to dance. The ladies, in turn, strategically positioned themselves in front of their desired partners. It all resembled a cat-and-mouse game, as women ducked to avoid certain men. One man, in particular, set himself up for rejection as he routinely wiped off his spectacles with his handkerchief before approaching a lady. Spotting his signal, the ladies quickly vanished. For women in general, it was preferable to be on the floor dancing rather than sitting as a wallflower, keeping in mind that there was only one 'Ladies Choice' for the entire evening. For many of the dance numbers, it was hardly necessary to have a dancing partner. As one fella put it, *"Ya could be jitterbugging around on the floor by yourself an devil the one would heed ya."* For the slow dance numbers, however, the scene was quite different. It was where couples hoped to 'square' romantically, as described in the following example:

*"Di ya come here often?"* was a standard opening line for a guy.

"It's my first time," the lady replied in a posh voice, even though she was a regular attendee.

*"Is the bifriend here?"* the guy continued.

"He's over there somewhere with his buddies," she lied. Continuing to dance around together, she singing along with the band and he contemplating his next move.

*"Can I buy ya a mineral?"*[35]

Depending on her interest in this guy, she either accepted or replied with a typical excuse, "I need to get back to my girlfriends."

With this lady, his chances seemed slim so it was best to move on with a final line, *"Buzz off, will ya!"*

As the evening progressed and the dance was nearing its end, couples could be seen dancing around cheek-to-cheek, leaving a dab of makeup and lipstick on the man's collar for his mother to wash off. She didn't mind this indeed if it meant that this son of hers had finally found a prospect for a wife

---

[35] A mineral was the term used for all soft drinks. They were served in the bars and dance halls, the more common being orange and lemonade.

to relieve herself, his *aul* mother, from some of the farm drudgery.

For me, the dances in Bonniconlon were like an extension of those held on the bridge. Many of the attendees were acquaintances. As such, courtesy dances were exchanged. At that time, I was a neophyte at ballroom dancing, with a tendency to lead rather than being led. On one occasion, in an effort to swing me around, the spiked heel of my shoe got caught in the cuff of my partner's trousers, sending us both swiftly to the floor for a new version of the tango. With no formal lessons, we learned to dance by ourselves with practice. For this reason, I was grateful when the opportunity presented itself so that I could improve my own dance movements. I also enjoyed attending the country hall dances in order to watch my neighbour's band perform live. Known as the Bobby McCafferty Band, it played regularly in the Bonniconlon hall with Bobby, his brothers and fellow musicians performing. This gifted group of self-trained musicians held their practice sessions outside the McCafferty home in Caltra Village, displaying their talent in music to the entire neighbourhood. Seeing them perform on stage, and dancing to their music, made the long bike ride worthwhile.

The dances continued until one or two o'clock in the morning, after which we faced the journey home. To our surprise, the Gardaí awaited us at our bicycles to ensure that all of our bikes had working lights, which was compulsory. The Gardaí were at a disadvantage, however, since they came from different regions of Ireland and did not know the local people. In addition, carrying identification was not a requirement. Taking advantage of both, we gave fictional names or, better yet, names of some characters from our villages. The fines were sent in the mail accordingly, stating, "Caught without a light on your bike while attending a dance in Bonniconlon on the night of …" When these bewildered misfortunates appeared in court with their summons in hand, the judge from his bench took one look at the 'dancing crew' on front of him and could only conclude that the entire country had gone mad, as he blessed himself while muttering "Jesus, Mary and Joseph!"

The clergy might also show up following a dance to make sure that, "No young girl got herself in trouble." With few automobiles, couples might be found romancing along the roadside where the clergy could have a word with them. In those days, it was the lady's responsibility to protect her virginity, since all brides should be virgins and most ladies wanted to be brides. For the unfortunate who missed out, all was not lost since she gained a fancy title of 'Old Maid' or 'Spinster' and for a so called 'Loose' woman, her accolade was 'Tramp' or 'Slut'. The 'Spinster' played an important role historically, spinning sheep's wool in the loft of the family home, thus the origin of her title. Somehow, I managed to escape this destiny in the loft.

*"Merrily cheerily noiselessly whirring*
*Swings the wheel spins the wheel while the foot's stirring*
*Sprightly and lightly and merrily ringing*
*Trills the sweet voice of the young maiden singing..."*

*Spinning Wheel* by David Clayton Thomas, 1941

Alas, her station in the loft now stands idle following the outsourcing of her job to foreign shores, freeing the maiden for similar useful jobs around the house.

In the case of a resulting pregnancy, the lady was often sent to an institution by her parents to avoid shame and embarrassment for the family. We have since learned about the scandals of the Magdalene Laundries and the unmarked graves in Ireland where unmarried mothers were forced to give up their babies as well as their lives. Run by religious orders and quietly supported by the State, the 'fallen' women were incarcerated for transgressing the conservative moral values of the time. Without ever having committed a crime, the penitent inmates suffered physically, spiritually and mentally.

Many ended up working in these asylums for the rest of their lives, providing free labour for these self-sustaining secretive operations. The responsible man, however, was not held accountable. His name was never mentioned, and he had no obligation for child support. It was the young woman's problem. The surviving babies were usually adopted with the aid of the clergy, as illustrated in the film *Philome*.

# 28

# Revolutionary Music

Following our introduction to ballroom dancing in Bonniconlon, my pals and I were ready to explore the more modern ballrooms that featured big band music and dance. This was the 1950s, the era of rock and roll music. The latest hits came to us via *Radio Luxembourg* and as teenagers, we made a point of learning the lyrics. My village pals then were Ann Ferguson and Teresa McNulty. They both loved to sing and were fun to hang around with. We enjoyed singing the hits together as we walked the roads or travelled to and from the dances. In particular, we liked Elvis, and tried to replicate his voice as we sung *Are You Lonesome Tonight, Wooden Heart, Jailhouse Rock* and *Love Me Tender*. At the same time, the Irish showbands were gaining popularity globally for their music and performances.

The most notable among them was The Royal Show Band, featuring Brendan Bowyer. Known for his Elvis impersonations, Brendan tailored American rock to his own Irish songs. He had several number one hits, of which I really liked *Hucklebuck Shoe,* and *I Walked All The Way Home*. His band, along with other Irish showbands, performed frequently around home.

The ballrooms competed for them, offering mid-week and Sunday night dances as advertised and promoted on regional newspapers. Staying abreast of them all and choosing which performances to attend, was normal. At the dances, we observed the bands perform on stage playing their own hits, and also those of leading artists such as Chuck Berry, Bill Haley, Fats Domino and the Everly Brothers, to name but a few. For jazz, they duplicated *Satchmo* to perfection, complete with the white handkerchief. These Irish showbands toured renowned entertainment centres where they were in demand, including Las Vegas. We were fortunate to dance to their music and to watch their live stage shows in our local ballrooms in rural Ireland.

# 29

# Ballroom Dancing

Getting ready for the the ballroom dance was an all-day affair for a young lady. The big band ballroom that I and my pals, Ann and Teresa, frequented was called the Marine Ballroom. It was located in the town of Inishcrone in County Sligo, a distance of about eight miles from home.[36] In order to get there, we hitchhiked on the main Sligo Road. This was a busy road with traffic, making it easy to get a lift. Since many other hitchhikers were already on the road, we strategically positioned ourselves at the start of the traffic. From there, we selected our target cars by their license plates, before sticking out our thumbs. Our ideal candidates were cars from out-of-town or those headed for the dance. Usually, it was raining, thus ruining our hair and our make-up before we ever reached the ballroom. Lucky for us ladies, there was adequate time to dry out inside the hall before the men showed up. They hung out in the pub until its closing time. In those days, ladies did not frequent pubs, instead we waited inside the ballroom dancing with each other to pass

---

[36] Inishcrone or *Inis Eascar Abhann* in Irish, means Island on the sandbank of the river.

the time. Then close to midnight, the men poured in, feeling merry from their pub drinks. Suddenly the ballroom came alive, as the band music increased in volume and the dancing couples took to the floor. We moved and swung to the latest hits, demonstrating our innate talent for modern dance, be it the twist, the jive, or the rock 'n roll.

> *"We're gonna do the twist and it goes like this:*
> *Come on, let's twist again like we did last summer,*
> *yeah, let's twist again like we did last year…"*

*Let's Twist Again* by Kal Mann and David Appell
Released as a song by Chubby Checker in 1961

We were in awe of the band and the music. But with a few hours remaining before the dance ended, one of us pals had to find a man with a car to take us home. Though each of us were attractive young women, Teresa, with her big blue eyes, could turn on the charm like none other. The lucky

guy, happy with his one 'score' for the evening, had a surprise coming as more women piled into his car. Fortunately, he was still feeling merry from visiting the pub, but once he realised what he was tasked with, he quickly sobered up.[37] Arriving home in the wee hours of the morning, we at times requested a drop

---

[36] In those days, legal standards on driving under the influence were not yet finalised due to the limited number of automobiles in the countryside.

123

off at a neighbour's house to avoid waking up our parents. It was better they did not know the hours we kept, and how we got to and from the dance. A problem arose, however, as the neighbour's dogs barked at the sound of the car, alerting the homeowner. Wondering about the traffic activity around his house in the early morning hours, he asked around. No one in the village had the answer except for the dancing trio, who remained silent about their shenanigans.

# 30

# The Dating Game

As teenagers we did not take dating too seriously. Most of us still lived at home, where there were no telephones or other means for remote communication. Arranging a date involved planning in advance by defining a specific meeting place and time, as described in the following memorable date: My friend Noreen had a secret admirer named Eamon, whom she met while dancing in Bonniconlon. Given the distance between their homes, they agreed to meet halfway at the statue in Whitestream, a village about three miles from home, and named after the stream running next to it. Somehow, Noreen arranged for me to come along on a blind date with Eamon's friend, Seamus. To get there we had just one bike that belonged to Noreen's father. Placing me on the handlebar, Noreen did the cycling, but I was taller than she making it necessary to lean back so that Noreen could see over my shoulder. Arriving at the Statue, it was raining so we stepped into a nearby cow shed with our dates for shelter. Inside, the cows lay chewing on their cud. Staring at us, it appeared as if the cows were trying to decipher which planet these strange aliens had dropped from to invade their territory. Finding opposite corners at the bottom of the shed, we stood with our dates sampling sweets they had taken along, but which had been crushed and became soggy from the rain. Any kisses exchanged were tinged with the scent of cow dung, thus putting a quick end to our romantic evening, with no chance for a future date.

While not all romantic dates were this thrilling, I recall seeing dating couples in search of privacy along the Caltra Road and sharing their sweets, while we children observed them from a distance. For formal evenings, couples went dancing or took in a film at the local cinema. The demand for films scaled during the furloughed dancing periods at Christmas and Lent, making the proprietors of the theatres happy with the surge. In spite of such limitations for dating in rural Ireland at that time, singles somehow connected in love and marriage, sealed at times with the Claddagh ring.[38] One only had to scan the social pages of the *Irish Independent* on Saturdays to read about the newly engaged couples or listen to the live radio show dedicated to the love birds to learn about their romances. Newlyweds liked to display their wedding photos in the local newspapers with their degrees and credentials, if any, listed after their names. Parents had little control over their children's spousal choice, very often falling out with them and refusing to attend their marriage service, especially when the marriages were of mixed religions. The custom of matchmaking had long since passed.

My dating experience around home was limited. For the few movie dates I had with men, I saw little of the film as I found myself sitting in a back row seat. Those seats were in high demand and occupied mainly with dating couples. Following the film, the two mile walk home in the dark, with my date escorting me, was enough to quench any romantic flame. My interaction with Irish men then was mostly flirtatious and role playing. Men did the pursuing, the asking and the treating, sometimes preceded with the odd wink or whistle, which were all accepted and considered complimentary for a

---

[38] The Claddagh ring dates from the 17th century. It originated in the fishing village of Claddagh in County Galway. The ring features a heart, a crown and hands as symbols for love, loyalty and friendship. This makes it an ideal engagement or wedding ring.

woman. Like many other young women of my day, I felt the need to explore further afield before settling down. This was the late 1950s when Irish women were establishing careers for themselves. Many of us went to the cities for further development and work, where we sought men with professional jobs in banking or in business. Such jobs brought steady incomes unlike farming. No longer were many Irish women interested in simply being farmers' wives. This left a scarcity of potential wives for young farmers. The saying, "You walk up the aisle with a full farm of land and you walk down with half," became less of a threat. In the west of Ireland, the situation grew so serious that the local clergy established a marriage bureau to match women from the cities with eligible local farmers. This did not work very well, leaving young farmers without wives and families to carry on the farming life. Today as those farmers pass from this earth, their farms lie idle and ready for sale. House after roofless house remains empty, like a ghost town or a deserted village.

# Part Nine

# Bringing Home the Bacon

# 31

# Markets and Fairs

Throughout rural Ireland, towns held market days or Fair Days as they were called, during which farmers traded livestock on the streets. Bargaining and bidding over prices was a standard practice. Once the deal closed, it was sealed with a spit and a strong handshake. Real money was exchanged, keeping the banks busy with cash deposits and withdrawals. Banking was a very private affair for farmers, as they stood carefully counting their money in a corner of the bank. With cap doffed, they looked all about to make sure no one was watching over their shoulder. At such times, they appreciated the fact that the bankers behind the counter were not local people. For professional reasons, bankers were stationed in regions far from their homes and regularly re-assigned to avoid cronyism. While the Fair Day was male oriented, women were on hand to watch over the money. For my family, a villager would volunteer his time and ability to negotiate the price and the resulting sale of our livestock since my brothers were then inexperienced in that role. Following a deal, pubs were kept busy as farmers stood each other a drink, while the wives tried to control the spending. In some cases, the proceeds from the cattle sales vanished due to extended drinking and outstanding pub debt enabled by the publicans, leaving the wives and children with no money. A Fair Day also brought out the Gypsy and the Tinker population who came to trade their horses and related goods. With a few pints consumed, they could be seen on the streets arguing and fist-fighting with each other. Around the corner, the Gardaí were on the beat with their batons in hand to intervene and to maintain order.

> "Trottin' to the fair, me and Molly Maloney,
> seated I declare on a single pony ..."

Trottin' to The Fair by Alfred Perceval Grav (1846-1931)

The flow of commerce touched every business in town on a Fair Day. Shoppers sought bargains in clothing, household goods and farming supplies as merchants displayed seasonal inventory at their front doors, promoting discounted pricing. Vendors with their open carts on the streets sold fresh vegetables, poultry, and seafood. The variety of seafood offered could be extensive, including mackerel, herring, dried kippers, cockles, mussels and seaweeds of carrageen moss and dillisk. Places to eat and drink were hopping with custom throughout the day, be it bar or restaurant. The Fair Day was a means of bringing the farming community and the town together in trade. While such markets had been an integral part of Irish tradition for centuries, few towns in Ireland today continue the practice, due to the introduction of the cattle mart in the late 1950s, resulting in greater efficiencies away from town centres.

My first time attending a Fair Day in Ballina was during my school years at *The Tech*. For me, it was an awakening to see such street activity. The sounds and the smells were intoxicating. I was disturbed by the cattle scene on the streets, knowing that they stood there for several hours away from their natural environment without food or water. At the end of the day, the streets were filthy, requiring major cleaning and disinfecting to return them to normality. For Ballina, what once was the old market square now features a memorial to Joe Biden, 46th President of the United States, in reference to his ancestral roots. The square also offers many shops, a supermarket, and a parking lot, in keeping with progress and the change over time.

# 32

# Grocery Shopping

$M$y earliest recollection of grocery shopping dates back to the post-war years when rationing was in effect. Introduced by the Irish government under

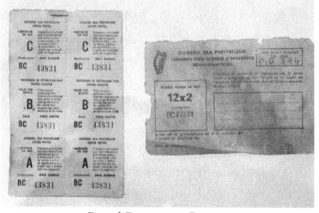

Petrol Rationing Coupon

the Emergency Powers Act, the rationing of food, clothes and petrol was enacted. This was followed by restrictions on shoes, soap and tobacco among other goods. To administer the process, ration books were issued to each family member with rules for tracking product sales, dates and place of purchase. I recall the image of my little ration book as I watched the shopkeeper, Mr. McNamara, stamp it on his countertop. Mam had established his shop for her grocery needs at that time. Among the food items rationed on her list were tea, sugar, butter and flour. As substitutes for tea and butter, Mam bought bottles of Irel coffee for a hot beverage and tins of *Lyles* golden syrup and treacle as a spread for our bread. I clearly remember the branding and packaging of those products and continue to associate them with rationing. Despite the restrictions, farming families around home considered themselves fortunate, since they could cultivate food on their lands. Mam continued to maintain her poultry and vegetable farms in those years, selling excess eggs and fowl to offset her grocery bill. However, the country man was at a loss without tobacco to fill his pipe and roll his cigarettes. As a poor substitute, he might try a puff or a pull on some dried leaves or even on a piece of turf.

In those days, shops in Ireland could only be found in towns and cities. They were mainly family-run small businesses, except for the Lipton chain that had stores across the country, specialising in high-end groceries. With limited access to shops, it was necessary for country folk to stock up on groceries in their homes. Should they run low, the custom of borrowing from neighbours was typical. This was especially true as unexpected visitors showed up, and it was customary to serve food to all guests. Sneaking out through their back entrance, the neighbour went next door to borrow extra rations or foods that could be spared for the occasion. For such needs in my home, Mam had an established relationship with the Ruddy family that lived across the road from us. In particular, I recall going back and forth between our two houses with cups filled with sugar and tea and other borrowed essentials. This custom of neighbourhood borrowing also extended to other household items needed at a given time, such as tools or even bicycles. All were returned and replenished in good faith and order. Alternatively, Mam might send me off on her bike to Ballina for a rushed order. As the messenger, I went to our customary shop where the order was fulfilled and lodged for later settlement allowing me to return home expeditiously with the goods.

Sadly, both the family-run business and the Lipton chain are now history. They have been forced out of business, unable to compete with the supermarket chains. For most rural women, grocery shopping in town was the highlight of their week. On such occasions, they dressed in their finest outfits complete with hat, gloves and high-heeled shoes. In the shop, they met up with friends and relatives. It was there where Mam frequently socialised with her relatives and friends while the shopkeeper, Myra O'Hora, compiled their grocery orders. This approach to grocery shopping remained in effect in my Ireland. Meeting up with friends, chatting with the shopkeeper, sharing a drink in the snug or a cup of tea in the back kitchen of the shop are no longer the norm. The large, self-service market along with the automobile in the parking lot, allow for greater efficiencies, thus ushering Ireland into the modern age.

# 33

# The Shop Girl

In the 1950s, the majority of teenagers in rural Ireland were expected to find paying jobs to help support the family at home. As such, I found employment in a hardware shop in Ballina. The business was owned and operated by three single brothers, Marty O'Malley and his younger twin siblings, Finn and Aidan.[39] Marty, short and stout, bossed the handsome twins around. Finn, who had a propensity for gambling, at times gambled away a day's proceeds from the business. This resulted in a row, with Marty chasing Finn around the shop, swinging blows, but missing his target as Finn ducked each time. From behind the counter, Marty loved to chat with customers, and his laughter could be heard on the street outside. As attractive female customers entered the shop, Marty turned on the charm, adopting a posh accent, and smiling all the while. Once they left, he often turned to me for reassurance with a question such as "Am I not a fine-looking fella?" To this, I once suggested that he take a peek in the looking glass to see for himself, hoping

---

[39] The characters are real but the names are disguised for privacy purposes and respect for the deceased and surviving family members.

that would put an end to his strange notions. He really did fancy himself as a 'lady killer.' One day, Marty was selling wallpaper to a lady customer. To retrieve the selection, it was necessary for him to climb up a ladder. In the reach, the ladder slipped from beneath, leaving Marty dangling from the shelf above. With legs swinging in search of the ladder, the swearing and cursing replaced the charm and posh accent, putting a damper on the sale of the wallpaper.

Although it was a hardware shop, it offered a broad range of products, covering household goods and decorations, furniture, luggage, men's shoes, and farm seeds. The products were well advertised, but the inventory in stock was sparse or non-existent. This management team believed in sample inventory where possible. For instance, a customer would see a sample shoe, "From a new shipment that had just arrived", though no such shipment existed. Instead, a messenger was sent on a bike to the wholesaler down the street to pick up a few similar shoe styles. Meanwhile, the customer waited patiently, wondering why it was taking so long to open up the shipment. Returning dishevelled from the bike ride, the messenger would hand the shoes to Marty, who resumed with the promotion in the hopes of a sale. If no sale resulted, the shoes were immediately returned to the wholesaler, thus avoiding surplus or stale inventory and related storage space. Marty was ahead of his time in inventory turnover. On one occasion, a man was talked into buying a pair of leather boots, with an assurance that, "These are the best boots you will find on the market, a hundred percent waterproof as guaranteed by the manufacturer." Once purchased, the customer discovered that the boots were not waterproof at all since the dampness soaked right through. Returning them to the shop, Marty was tasked with sending them back to the manufacturer. Instead, the boots remained under the counter for weeks, while the customer continued to check on their status. Eventually, to resolve the problem, Marty dipped the boots in a barrel of linseed oil at the shop. Returning them to the customer, Marty pretended that they had come back from the manufacturer, and were once again, "The best *fecking* boots on the market, waterproof guaranteed." Within a week, the boots found their way back to the shop to haunt Marty as he flung them under the counter once again ready for the next dance session and a fresh dip in the barrel of linseed oil.

A major problem arose when a farmer, who was also a relative of the O'Malley brothers, arrived in town with his donkey and cart to pick up his order of farm seed, as promised by Marty. With no fulfilment of the order, Marty blamed the supplier. Not accepting this excuse, the farmer, in a rage, lifted his fists, swearing and threatening, "O'Malley, where's my *fecking* oats, you *bleddy* bastard?" Bolting from the shop, the farmer untethered his donkey from the pole outside and headed for home, still in a rage. It appeared as though the farmer's day was wasted, since he gave himself an early start in the hopes of sowing his oat seed that same day. But not all was lost. By the end of the day, Marty had made good on his promise by replacing the order and delivering it to the farmer's doorstep. Such were the challenges of doing business with relatives and neighbours in a tight community, where loyalty and friendships were paramount.

The shop was long and narrow, displaying dishes and gift items on shelves that were not very secure. A few accidents occurred, resulting in inventory write-offs. The worst happened during a Fair Day in Ballina, when a bullock dashed into the shop from the street. Unable to turn around, the animal crashed into both sides, sending dishes and glassware flying. To get the bull out, it was necessary for its owner to grab its hind legs and drag, while

Marty faced the bull head on, backing him out. With arms in motion, Marty resembled a maestro conducting an orchestra, cheered on by the applause from

the spectators gathered on the street outside. Following this incident, a half-door was erected to keep all wild animals and wild people out.

Based on the variety of products offered, the O'Malley shop was kept busy with traffic. In this sense it was unique, since most stores in town specialised in a given product line. Marty was a born salesman. If the product was not in stock, he would find it elsewhere, with the promise to have it delivered free of charge. Delivery, however, meant delegating the role to an employee, with the expectation that the employee would use his or her personal bike. Marty assumed that staff bikes were at liberty for shop use, without consideration of cost and maintenance. In addition to the service offered, the O'Malley store was friendly and inviting. People dropped by merely to chat with Marty and with each other. This was particularly true on Saturday evenings, when business hours were extended until 8PM, drawing many shoppers to town. At such times, Marty was in his element entertaining them all, which may help to explain why his business shenanigans were tolerated. Among the frequent visitors was a Johnny Curry, a short man sporting a moustache and carrying a shillelagh walking stick. Johnny spent his adult life looking for a wife. Although in his eighties, the search continued. With a twinkle in his eye, every woman that walked by got the 'once over' as a prospect, leading us to finally ask, "Do you think you'll find the wife in this life or in the life hereafter?" Johnny never gave up.

The O'Malley brothers also owned a travelling grocery business to serve the neighbouring countryside. It was operated out of a van that was fitted with shelving and storage to accommodate the fragile goods. Packing the van to full capacity was essential to maximise business and meet the needs of the area covered. This arm of the business was managed by Aidan, the second twin, who was most responsible and professional. Occasionally, I travelled with him. Starting early in the morning, we packed the van and planned for a long day in the countryside. Along the way, both buying and selling took place, as fresh farm products were exchanged for certain groceries. Specialty orders for household items also were fulfilled, since these customers were remote from town shops for such purchases. Throughout the day, much conversation took place as news about town and country was exchanged. As expected, invitations were extended for tea and treats as we went from village to village with our travelling van. I could relate to this side of the business, since it served country folk, and the products we purchased were fresh from the farms. The customer base was well established due to the lack of transportation to towns, the reliability of the van service with its standard grocery supply, and the absence of competing services. The O'Malley travelling van was ahead of its time, a precursor of future trends. If only Marty had a crystal ball to see orders placed with the click of a key and home delivery provided by a self-driven auto or by a drone, *there'd be no stoppin' him.'*

I continued to live at home for the two-year duration of my employment with the O'Malley brothers. The daily bike commute was reasonable, except in the bad weather of rain, wind, hail and cold. The shop was unheated, apart from an electric heater behind the counter, which was 'borrowed' from inventory, yet remained listed as a sale item. In the winter months, we gathered around the heater to stay warm, but later suffered from the resulting chilblains on both our hands and feet. We worked a standard forty-five-hour week with Thursday as a half day. In those days, there was no regulation in effect on working conditions and time off. At the shop, meals were provided as part of the package. The tiny kitchen at the rear was handy for breaks, and it served to keep us on the premises throughout the day. This concept can be compared with modern corporate culture, where food is supplied to employees to maintain continuous productivity. For me, working such hours left little time for extra-curricular activities. But then, there was little spending money for such, since the bulk of my skimpy pay was used to help run the family farm.

While the O'Malley shop was my first experience in the work force, at times I was unsure if I had landed at a legitimate business or at an amusement house. During my time there, I did learn some business fundamentals. High on the list was customer service, followed by product diversification for all seasons and inventory management, but not the 'Marty' style. My relationship with the O'Malley brothers was friendly. They included me in their extended family where I got to know their mother, sisters, brothers and cousins. Since most of us were single, we frequented the local ballrooms where we exchanged courtesy dances. At all times, whether it be work or pleasure, I was referred to as Miss Connor in keeping with my employee status. Eventually, I took my leave to seek a career in the hospitality industry, a setting that incorporated certain aspects of my business training, in particular customer relations and service with a smile.

Immediate male members of my family

Immediate female members of my family

Part Ten

# Leaving Home

# 34

# Youthful Ambitions

Our mother wanted all of her children to stay around home. She was of the old mindset that boys ran the farm and girls were married off locally, thus providing continuity and care for the elderly. But her children had minds of their own. Both Jim and Francie had left home to pursue their individual careers by the time I was a teenager. I was the next in the family to leave the nest. Mam was not supportive of our leaving, disagreeing with each of our plans as she pointed out and focused on the negatives. Yet, she was later proud of our accomplishments once we were established. Her life was changing. Her struggles to raise her four children were over.

> *"Tis the last rose of summer left blooming alone.*
> *All her lovely companions are faded and gone*
> *No flower of her kindred, no rosebud is nigh*
> *To reflect back her blushes and give sigh for sigh ..."*

*The Last Rose of Summer* by Thomas Moore (1779-1852)

My decision to leave for Dublin was my own. While most of my peers were going across the English Channel to better their lives, I remained committed to Ireland believing that it offered adequate career options. Women's opportunities then were mainly in nursing, teaching and business. I was especially attracted to the hotel profession. This was a popular career track in Ireland for both men and women, given the strong tourist industry in the country. Since Dublin offered the greatest choices, I was pleased to identify and be accepted into a hands-on training programme at the Grand Hotel in Dublin. Packing my few possessions in a wee suitcase, a farewell gift from the hardware shop, I added a small bottle of holy water for good luck. Then, with little money to get to Dublin, I arranged for a lift with my friend, Des McAndrew. He travelled to the city frequently on business and could drop me off enroute at my Dublin destination. Des, a handsome and bright young lad, worked at his father's garage in Ballina. He and I became acquainted while attending the dances around home. Occasionally, we met up in Dublin during my years there, where we shared a snack or a drive around the city exploring various neighbourhoods. Ours was a teenage attraction that developed into a permanent friendship though we went on separate paths through life. As a souvenir, Des left me with some post-war petrol rationing forms related to his garage which I cherish and include as part of my story.

# 35

# Hotel Training

$A$t the age of eighteen, I began my training for hotel management at the Grand Hotel in Malahide, Dublin.[40] The hotel was majestically located overlooking an estuary on the Irish Sea. It was built in the 1800s by James Fagan who was a member of the English Parliament. Originally called the Royal Hotel, its name was changed in the early 1900s following the reawakening of Irish nationalism. During World War One, the hotel was chosen as the Irish headquarters for the British army, in anticipation of a German invasion. After the war, the building was refurbished to operate again as a hotel. During my time living in Dublin, the Grand offered a range of hospitality services. In addition to accommodation, dining and bar, the hotel catered to banquets, weddings and dinner dancing to live music. The functions were formal, with ladies and gents dressed in their finest, displaying style and elegance.

---

[40] The word Malahide, or *Mullach-ide* in Irish, meaning the Hill of Hyde, is believed to have been named after a Norman family. Located on the Irish Sea about ten miles north of Dublin City, the town has a rich history, covering the landing of the Vikings in 795 to the arrival of the Anglo-Normans in the 12th century. Its ancient castle remains a tourist attraction. The town has grown significantly since my day.

The two-year management programme at the hotel was intense. Trainees rotated around departments to learn the entire business. For me, the catering part was the most interesting. It entailed planning and strategy, while also allowing for creativity. I learned the importance of capacity guidelines relative to floor space for a given venue together with table layout and table positioning. The set-up styles could vary from U-shape to banquet or conference, among others. For outdoor receptions on the lawn, the style was always stand-up. I helped with the flower arrangements, the silver and crystal placements and the napkins shaped like the Pope's hat, into which we dropped the bread rolls. Dressed in traditional black and white attire, I participated at numerous receptions serving *hors d'oeuvres* from silver platters. I also served drinks of port and sherry in their wee glasses from silver trays, while at the same time listening to and enjoying the live music of the string quartets playing Haydn, Mendelssohn, or Vivaldi. At times, I was assigned a role as an attendee at wedding functions. In the midst of the celebration, I took pleasure in delivering the many telegraphs that arrived for the newlyweds and in hearing their amusing messages as read aloud by the master of ceremonies. This was followed with speeches and song from guests around the tables, including the popular wedding song *Our Lovely Day*, that required the voice of a soprano to reach the high notes.[41] Having heard it sung at different weddings, I became familiar with the lyrics and will always associate this song with the Grand Hotel.

*"This is my lovely day,*
*This is the day I shall remember the day I'm dying.*
*They can't take this away,*
*It will be always mine, the sun and the wine,*
*The sea birds crying…"*

*My Lovely Day* with music by Vivian Ellis and book
and lyrics by A. P. Herbert.

---

[41] The song is from the musical *Bless the Bride* produced in London in 1947. It has remained a popular wedding song.

While the cuisine was traditional Irish at the Grand Hotel, I had much to learn from the all-male team of chefs. Already knowledgeable about the basic methods of cooking meats, fish and vegetables from home, at the hotel I learned ways to enrich flavours through searing and braising, simmering and seasoning, together with heat types to maximise tenderness and nutrients. In my role as trainee, I mastered the baking of Yorkshire pudding to serve with roast beef. I also expanded my knowledge of dessert recipes for flans, puddings, pies, tarts, trifle and baked or stewed fruits, all served with complementary custards, creams and sauces. The hotel hosted many evening events, including dinner dances in the winter months. As the dancing wound down around midnight, it was customary to serve hot soup together with a drink of choice. Of the many drinks offered, I took pride in the preparation of an Irish coffee by adhering to the delicate steps in its making. The final step, however, was the most critical. It involved pouring unwhipped fresh cream over the back of a spoon so that the cream floated smoothly on top of the coffee, representing a work of art for presentation. This was the most satisfying night cap for me to end a workday in the kitchen.

In the formal dining room, laid out with white linen tablecloths and napkins, I was introduced to silver service. From a large silver platter placed on my arm, I learned to use the relevant utensils to serve the food from the platter onto the guests' plates. I also mastered the art of carrying multiple plates on one arm to and from the tables, while serving food from the left and clearing dishes from the right. The headwaiter, dressed in tails complete with white gloves, was ever present, directing the workflow. At banquets, he signalled to us waiters and waitresses on the timing of courses so that we all moved in unison serving each table. The clicking and clacking of the dishes drowned out the live music and conversation in the room. It was a lovely sight to see the serving staff dressed in their black and white uniforms as they marched to and from the kitchen, resembling a family of penguins. On the banquet table at the end of the room was a food display consisting of, among others, a large salmon on a silver platter with a lemon in its mouth and a suckling pig's head with an apple between its teeth. It was all so impressive and particularly so to a young girl from rural Ireland.

During my two-year training at the Grand Hotel, I learned the importance of full-capacity room reservations, an active restaurant and bar business, and an ongoing roster for private functions. I came to realise that this meant attracting customers with competitive pricing, quality service and venue options for special events. At the same time, I understood the relevance of cost containment for better profit margins. While financials reveal the success of any business, I became educated on the importance of managerial skills and appropriate staffing, since they are the forces that make it all happen. I got to know many fine people during those two years at the Grand, from management to staff and to fellow trainees.

One of the most amusing was a bartender at the hotel, named Frank. He was convinced that he was a Humphrey Bogart double, reminding all of us about the likeness. While Frank did indeed resemble the American cultural idol, he personified the image when smoking a cigarette and wearing a trench coat and hat. His efforts to perfect Bogart's unique speech patterns and distinctive voice with its trademark lisp, was the challenge. For this, Frank practiced various forms of lip gymnastics, grins and nasal tones, keeping us colleagues highly entertained. For the duration of my training at the Grand Hotel, my best pal was Mary Byrne from County Roscommon. We went through the programme together, becoming staunch buddies from the start. We were lucky in that our schedules for duty and leisure coincided, allowing us to plan together. As newcomers to Dublin, we wanted to explore the county and could get around by public transportation. In the summer months, our preference was to explore seaside towns such as Dun Laoghaire, Howth and Bray. In such places, we could lay on the strand in the hopes of getting a tan. It was fashionable in Ireland those days to flaunt a tan, an indication of having vacationed on the Continent at resorts in Spain or in Greece. Since both Mary and I were fair skinned, our tanning efforts left us with severe sunburns, resulting in layers of skin peeling off our backs. As a substitute for a real tan, we tried a tanning lotion, but quickly learned of its limitations, since most of it ended up on our clothes, leaving us with a zebra-like body tan. That put an end to my attempts at trying to turn my white skin brown. During the winter months, Mary and I focused on Dublin City where we shopped for clothes and took in some fine films like *The Ten Commandments*, *Inherit the Wind* and *Gigi*. Having a companion to share those extracurricular activities as well as the hotel training, made my introduction to Dublin exceptional. As two farm girls from the West, we had much in common. Mary, a tall well-built girl with a cheerful disposition, loved to talk about her family and her life in Roscommon. It was not surprising that, at the end of our programme, Mary sought and obtained an opportunity close to her home. Lastly, the Grand Hotel had a riding school and stables on its grounds. The school drew much business from both the hotel guests and the surrounding areas. It was well staffed with riding instructors and caretakers. From time-to-time we trainees were invited, as a bonus, to ride together with an instructor. This was very special for me as it reminded me of Tom, our horse at home. Sitting side-saddle in my skirted outfit, I felt such joy riding horse-back along the broad golden strand that stretched for miles beside the Irish Sea.

# 36

# Working in Dublin

Following my two-year hotel training programme, I took a position as an officer at the Four Courts Hotel in Dublin City. The hotel was located on Inns Quay, next to Ireland's main court building that originally housed the four courts of Chancery.[42] Though the hotel no longer stands, it was on a par with its neighbour, The Ormond Hotel, in terms of size and business model. My principal role at the Four Courts Hotel was that of purchasing and supply management. This covered standard hotel operations as well as special functions such as banquets and weddings. This meant being aware of events in Dublin to ensure having adequate supplies in house for potential business. Starting with the booking register, I noted the chosen menus, including the selected wines and spirits. With this information in hand, my day began by consulting with each department head for their supply lists based on the

---

[42] Inns Quay is on the banks of the River Liffey. It has played an important role in Dublin's history. Dating back to the 13th century, Inns Quay was developed as a shipping centre under the British Crown. It continued as such until the 1800s when its waters were considered too shallow for the larger, heavy ships. Inns Quay, together with the other Dublin quays, intersect Dublin City with the bridges of the Liffey, offering a scenic view of the city.

known and anticipated trade. Next, I met with the hotel manager, a tall, charming Englishman who lived on the premises with his Italian wife and family. Together, we reviewed the information gathered before finalising our procurement plan. Placing the orders with various suppliers around the city, I routinely negotiated for the highest quality at the best price. As the deliveries arrived, it was necessary to qualify and sign off on each before storing the goods. For this step I employed a store man, named Freddy, who assisted me by keeping an eye on the deliveries until I arrived with the keys to lock them up. It was like having the keys to the kingdom, with so many of them on one chain. Freddy proved to be a loyal staff member who covered for me during my disappearances on personal errands. As a show of gratitude, I would pay him in advance by slipping his envelope through the sliding window of the office upon hearing his knock. Later when I had left the hotel to work abroad, I would send Freddie a Christmas card with a few dollars inside, only to receive back a box of embroidered handkerchiefs, a popular gift for ladies at that time.

As keeper of the cellar, I became educated about wines, liqueurs and spirits in general. In those years, the availability of wines and liqueurs in Ireland was somewhat limited and required specialty orders through distributors. At first, I had difficulty trying to pronounce the names, *Beaujolais, Châteauneuf-du-Pape, Liebfraumilch* among others, as displayed on the labels of the French, German and other continental bottles. Managing such stock was challenging in order to meet demand yet avoid excess inventory on the shelves. For spirits and beer, however, the demand was constant and the supply readily available since most came from local dealers. In compliance with accounting requirements, I maintained an inventory tracking system that was audited every calendar quarter by an outside audit firm. Likewise, on a weekly basis, I reconciled accounts payable against delivered supplies before hand-writing the cheques, and then leaving them for the manager to review and sign. In essence, I was the manual accountant for the hotel, predating the automation of an accounting and cheque processing system. This hands-on experience taught me the fundamentals in accounting which proved valuable for my later career in that discipline.

A welcome diversion from my core duties was that of default manager for my fellow officials during their absences. This allowed me to work around the hotel with other staff members. Briefed and knowledgeable about the tasks involved, I could substitute easily as needed. When it came to overseeing the workflow from the laundry room to the bedrooms, my day began with an early start. From a locked closet, I distributed clean linen while the housemaids gathered around loading up their carts with fresh laundry to take to their assigned floors. The all-female staff of varying ages dressed in blue uniform with white apron and bonnet, worked different shifts during the day. Problems arose for family emergencies, causing me to shuffle schedules and question the validity of the emergencies since they occurred frequently on my assigned days. With checkout time for guests set at noon, the housemaids had limited time to clean and prepare the rooms for new arrivals. This was especially true when large tour groups were booked which was frequent at the Four Courts. Arriving in busloads, the tourists crowded into the hotel lobby as the bellhops carried the suitcases from the bus and then loaded them onto the luggage carts for designated room deliveries. The resulting commotion was extreme, especially when the tourists were American. Their voices resonated around the hotel as they sought service and complained about the cold. For new arrivals, I checked each room in advance, getting much exercise as I went from floor to floor and from room to room. One housemaid would hide upon hearing my footsteps. Knowing her game, I too would hide until I heard her movements and then suddenly appear in front of her. We had an unusual working relationship, to say the least. I also had to contend with the hotel manager's wife who rushed around checking the work. This short Italian woman with much hair rolled up into a big bun, was frequently on the 'war path.' She spoke in broken English with a strong Italian accent augmented with arm movements in the air. Never fully understanding her, it occurred to me to also play the hiding game upon hearing her in the distance calling out in search of Miss Connor. What was important for me as the substitute manager, was to satisfy the duties of the hotel, and ensure a smooth handover to the official department head.

At the Four Courts Hotel, the officers, or officials as we were called, were a team of unwed females from different parts of Ireland and with diverse backgrounds. Among my fellow officers were Betty, Bridie, Mary, Nancy, Noreen, Peggy and Vera. Some of us had gone the university route, others were from professional families such as bankers, and I was the farm girl from Mayo. Our on-duty outfits were compulsory black at all times, creating a professional appearance. To the rest of the hotel staff, we were addressed as Miss before our surname, in keeping with the formality of our roles. Being an officer meant very special treatment. In our private living quarters at the hotel, we were provided with daily maid service, and we were not expected to make up our own beds in the morning. Should we become ill, we stayed in bed all day with a fire burning in our room for warmth. Our meals were taken to us on linen draped trays with a teapot covered by a cosy, accompanied by hot water in a silver pot, toast layered in a silver toast rack and a soft-boiled egg in its cup wearing a cap to keep it warm. For a flu or a cold, the cure was a hot toddy from the bar, consisting of good Irish whiskey or a pint of Guinness, believed to contain many nutrients. For regular meals, we were served in the formal dining room, complete with white linen tablecloths and silver settings. Our menu was similar to that offered to the hotel guests. Unlike the rest of the hotel staff, we could use the switchboard for personal phone calls and meet with our friends in the public lounges. This was important for me since I had many visitors from the West. It was great when my brothers showed up with their buddies after attending a football match in Croke Park. On such occasions, I would treat them all to a meal in the hotel dining room. They usually ordered steak and onions topped off with a whiskey or a bottle of stout to sustain them for their long drive home. As officers, we were carefully safeguarded. Permission to stay out late was a requirement, for which a late-night pass was granted, even though some of us were as old as Methuselah. This class and protective system must have been a throwback to English customs, as would later be depicted in the drama *Upstairs, Downstairs*.

# 37

# Exploring Dublin City

Dublin was my first city experience and it was a cultural awakening for me. Known for theatre excellence, I attended performances at the Abbey, the Gate and the Gaiety where I saw selections from the works of Beckett, Casey, Friel, Shaw and Wilde. The city also offered many cinemas, where I enjoyed great films such as *Ben-Hur*, *Spartacus,* and *West Side Story*. Accompanied by colleagues from the hotel, we stood at the start of each film for the Irish national anthem and waited until intermission for refreshments. At the end of the show, we treated ourselves to either Chinese soup or Wimpy burgers, since they offered the only fast food that we knew of in Dublin at that time.[43] The aroma from the grills whetted our appetites to indulge. Alternatively, we might decide on a selection of Danish pastries from Findley's bakery to take back to our residence at the Four Courts. Along the way, we often stopped to view some store windows and watch the new medium of television brought to Ireland in the late 1950s. The broadcasting services were then limited to

---

[43] Though Wimpy originated in the U.S. in the 1930s, the chain only reached the British Isles in the 1950s.

Britain (BBC) and Ulster (UTV), pending the introduction of Ireland's *Telefís Éireann* in the early 1960s. Returning to our residence at night-time, we habitually jumped on a bus. The red double-decker busses ran frequently, throwing off diesel fumes in the process. They were the only means of public transportation available in Dublin then. Climbing to the upper deck of the bus, we observed the city life as the bus conductor collected our fares. He rattled his strapped purse for attention and then issued us tickets from a wee machine he carried. Not knowing who got on or off the bus at each stop, he ran up and down the stairs relying on the passengers' honesty to pay their fares. Arriving at our stop, we prepared to jump off while the bus remained in motion. We only took the bus at night, as a precautionary measure. It was advantageous to explore the city by foot, which was fairly easy given its compactness, with most of the top attractions concentrated in the city centre.

In addition to socialising with colleagues from work, I developed new friends and reconnected with others. Among them was Philo Gallagher and her brother Aodh, schoolmates from Behy school. Both were then living in Dublin, Philo as a student in chemistry and Aodh advancing his skills in craftsmanship and carpentry. We got together periodically for flicks and outings to the seashore. On one occasion following an afternoon in Dun Laoghaire, we went to see the film *Cat on a Hot Tin Roof* starring Elizabeth Taylor and Paul Newman. It was an introduction for me to Tennessee William's writings and to U.S. southern life. The film sparked my curiosity about the author, leading me to later enjoy several live stage productions of his works and at the same time gaining an appreciation for his talent and culture. Through Philo I met her friend, Finola, a tall, elegant lady who worked for the civil service department in Dublin. She and I became close friends, sharing cultural and social events in the city. I vividly recall the evening we stood in line for some time outside the Delphi Theatre to see the film *Wuthering Heights*, enduring the cold and rain and the cigarette smoke around us. The film was a rerun of the original 1939 classic, starring Merle Oberon and Laurence Olivier. Our effort to see the movie version of Emily

Brontë's only novel, considered an English literature masterpiece, was very worthwhile. Viewing the scene of Yorkshire with its remote windswept moors, reminded me of the west of Ireland. This made me wonder what frame of mind the author was in when writing the turbulent tale of passion. Was it the isolation of the landscape that inspired the imagination of Emily and also that of her sisters, Charlotte and Anne, to write their famous novels? After seeing the picture, I was motivated to later walk in their footsteps through the trails of the Yorkshire moorland. Apart from taking in cultural events, Finola and I at times went dancing at the Metropole ballroom located on O'Connell Street. This landmark site dates back to the late 1800s where once stood the Georgian Metropole Hotel. In my day, the structure had been rebuilt as a neoclassic entertainment centre offering a cinema, bar and restaurant and a dancehall. The popular ballroom attracted national patrons and international visitors. It was where I first socialised with non-Irish persons, and it was a broadening experience for me. For quieter evenings, Finola and I oftentimes just read poetry aloud in her one-room flat in the city. That flat had special meaning for me since it was there where I spent my last night before leaving Ireland for the first time to venture abroad, with Finola seeing me off at Dublin Airport.

While it was preferable to have companionship for sharing Dublin's highlights, it was not always feasible due to work schedules and commitments. Consequently, I often found myself exploring alone given my curious nature. As a self-guided tourist, my explorations on foot continued with O'Connell Street, Dublin's main thoroughfare. This broad boulevard featured several neoclassic buildings housing banks and retail shops. Most notable among them was Clerys Department Store, with its two-faced clock over the main entrance.[44] Famous as a meeting place, it was where I also met up with friends for a rendezvous in the city.

Standing there, I had a clear view of Dublin's Pillar rising tall in the centre of the boulevard. This large granite monument, capped with the statue

---

[44] Established in 1853, it is believed to have been one of the world's oldest department stores.

of Horatio Nelson, was built to honour Nelson's victory at Trafalgar in 1805. Completed in 1809 when Ireland was politically part of the United Kingdom, it remained an important landmark in the city in my day. Though I never got to climb the Pillar's internal staircase to reach the viewing platform, I did note the bullet marks on the column resulting from Irish uprisings. The Pillar remained very controversial, particularly as Irish nationalist sentiment grew. Yet, it stood for more than 150 years as a prominent monument in the centre of Dublin city.

Close to the Pillar stood the General Post Office (GPO), one of Ireland's most famous buildings.[45] As well as being Ireland's main postal service, it also provided certain financial services, such as pensions and banking. It was there where I opened up my first savings account. Each month, I made a special trip to the GPO to deposit a few pounds from my wages. I took pride in watching my balance grow, as the male clerk behind the counter stamped my savings book and passed it back through the caged window. In those days, individuals did not have current accounts for cheque writing or credit cards for shopping. Instead, we paid in cash as we purchased, saving the balance left over for a rainy day. In the large open postal hall of the GPO, I admired the polished timber counters with brass grilles and the post boxes with brass embellishments, established for public use. Also noteworthy for me was the iron balustrade on the mezzanine level and the bronze sculpture of the legendary Irish hero, *Cú Chulainn*, at the central window. Exiting from the GPO onto Henry Street, one of Dublin's principal shopping districts, I would head for Moore Street.[46]

Moore Street, located off Henry Street, but somewhat hidden, is a cultural treasure and a famous landmark. It also is an original open-air street market established in the 1800s. At first glance, it reminded me of a market

---

[45] Dating back to the 1800s, the GPO is one of the last Georgian public buildings erected in the capital. During the Easter Uprising of 1916, it was laid waste by fire, leaving only the façade of the structure standing.
[46] Both Henry Street and Moore Street were named after Henry Moore, an 18th century developer and politician.

day in Ballina, except that this was a daily market with many more vendors selling their merchandise. The traders were mostly Irish natives then, many of whom were descendants from a long line of local merchant traders. Their thick Dublin accents and sharp-tongued wit was their true identity. They stood next to their shanty stalls, keeping a close eye on their goods, making it clear that there were no freebies to be had. Walking amidst the stalls set up in the middle of the street, I noticed the variety of fruits and vegetables for sale. As a farm girl, I could tell that some of the produce had seen better days, though delivered daily by horse-drawn cart from the suppliers. There, I sought seasonal fruits to eat and fresh flowers to brighten up my room back at the hotel. Bargaining for price was customary. The stallholders promoted their bargains with raised voices, "Apples, oranges, bananas going for a few pence," or, "Fresh lettuce, cabbage, carrots bundled together for a *quid*." The women traders showed up daily with curling pins or rollers in their hair covered over with a scarf, making me wonder where they were headed after work.

> *"In Dublin's fair city where the girls are so pretty,*
> *I first set my eyes on sweet Molly Malone,*
> *As she wheeled her wheelbarrow*
> *Through streets broad and narrow*
> *Crying 'cockles and mussels alive, alive, oh!' …"*

*Molly Malone* by James Yorkston (1876)


In addition to the stalls and carts, Moore Street itself was lined with small houses, many in need of structural repairs. Yet, in their midst one could find a traditional Irish bakery or a family-run butcher shop or even a fish shop selling the fresh catch of the day. It was an experience for me to visit Moore Street. No matter what hour of the day, the stallholders were friendly and ready to chat, hoping to make a sale. But trying to understand the local jargon before settling on the amount, be it in crowns or half-crowns, *bobs* (shillings) or *quids* (pounds), was the challenge. They were truly a unique cast of characters, with their antics, body language and lingo, that contributed to the charm of Moore Street.

Before leaving the north side of the city, I liked to stop by Easons on O'Connell Street. This book chain was eclectic in its offerings, as expressed by its catchy slogan, "So many reasons to shop at Easons." Though book censorship was then in effect in Ireland, with many Irish authors' works banned for 'indecency,' there was still much to choose from. At Easons, I always browsed for some time through newspapers, magazines, and books before making my selection. I also purchased my stationery and postcards there to correspond with family and friends, since this was our only means of remote communication. Satisfied with such outings in Dublin's north side, I would return to my residence by walking along the Liffey on Inns Quay, protecting my purchases from the weather. Later in my room, I dealt with my white undergarments turned black from the smoke and fumes of the city. As skirted women, keeping our lingerie from discolouration was impossible due to the thickened smog caused by the coal burning fireplaces of homes and businesses.

On other days, I continued on foot to explore Dublin's south side, on the opposite side of the Liffey. Crossing the river on O'Connell's Bridge, my stride was usually interrupted by a photographer snapping my picture with his sophisticated camera. While curious to see the developed copy, which could be a nice souvenir of Dublin, I deferred knowing that this photographer was ever present on O'Connell's Bridge promoting his business through the lens of his camera. In the centre of the bridge, I observed the Garda on point duty. Elevated in his booth, he directed the flow of traffic from all sides with his whistle and his white-gloved hands. Adding to the ambiance were the street musicians playing traditional Irish music, often as a duet, on their combined fiddle and banjo instruments. The melodies of their selected jigs and reels echoed through the wind. Once across the bridge in the direction of College

Green, I occasionally encountered a political rally.[47] This three-sided plaza was a popular assembly point for such gatherings. It was there where I saw, for the first time, some *Ban Gardaí* (this title for female Gardaí was discontinued in 1990 for being too gender specific). They walked in pairs in their skirted uniforms and were new to the force since *Ban Gardaí* recruiting only began in the late 1950s. The plaza, with its landmark buildings, drew many visitors and sightseers.

On the north side of the Green stood the Bank of Ireland headquarters.[48] This impressive structure appeared overwhelming to me, owing to its size, semi-circular shape, and colonnaded entrance. From reading about it, I understood that it was originally built to house the Irish Parliament, and that the second chamber remained intact and open to the public. Taking the tour, I viewed the coffered ceiling and decorative motifs of the interior. For me, however, the most important sight was the large tapestry depicting the Battle of the Boyne, which I had studied at Behy school.[49] The outside of the complex drew many artists displaying their talent, some of whom created drawings on the pavement itself. Also positioned outside the bank were newspaper vendors. They stacked their papers against the wall of the building, covering them over with a plastic to keep them dry. These vendors promoted their inventory by drawing attention to the latest headlines. Their messages were impossible to understand, however, as they rattled off important news in their local vernacular, thus adding to the city's buzz.

---

[47] College Green was originally known as Hoggen Green, from the Norse word *Haugr*, meaning mound. As such, it is believed that the burial mounds in the cemetery contain the remains of certain Norse kings of Dublin.

[48] This imposing structure, designed by Sir Edward Pearce, dates back to the 18th century, and was built to house the Irish Parliament. It is reported to have been the world's first bicameral parliament, consisting of a House of Commons and a House of Lords.

[49] The battle took place in 1690 between the forces of William lll, known as 'William of Orange', King of England, Scotland and Ireland and those of the deposed King James ll. Fought at the River Boyne in Ireland, William's resulting victory allowed for the continuation of Protestantism in Ireland. The victory is celebrated annually on the twelfth of July by the Protestant Orange Order in Ulster.

Across the street to the east side of the Green, is Trinity College, Dublin.[50] I already knew that it was Ireland's oldest surviving university and was world renowned, so I was excited about viewing it. From Parliament Square, I could see the iconic campanile, the chapel and the imposing old library, home to the famous *Book of Kells*.[51] I joined the queue once that lead to the rare and ancient manuscripts, and also the medieval Gaelic harp of Trinity College. While visiting Trinity Dublin with its housed treasures, its impressive buildings and its beautiful grounds was a novel experience, attending such an institution seemed totally out of reach for me. In my Ireland a university education was for the rich and the privileged. Around Trinity, I observed the students, formally dressed and carrying attaché cases. Most were male and many were students from abroad. This was my first time seeing dark-skinned people, since I had not yet been outside of Ireland and the rural population had remained homogenous and white.

Continuing on my explorations of Dublin's heritage, I later visited the Castle.[52] As a self-guided tourist, I viewed the great Record Tower, the only remaining building from the medieval fortification that once stood on this site. From there I walked to the gardens and stood on the spot of the once black pool, *Dubh linn* in Irish, from which Dublin got its name. Inside the buildings, I toured the richly decorated private quarters and entertaining halls, and the Chapel Royal. I ended my tour in the under croft, where a part of the

---

[50] Founded in the 16th century by Queen Elizabeth 1st, it was modelled after the Oxford and Cambridge university colleges, though only one college was established at Trinity Dublin. Built as a Protestant institution, it remained so for most of its history, since the Irish Catholic clergy, in turn, restricted Catholics from attending.

[51] *The Book of Kells* is an illuminated, medieval manuscript, documenting the Four Gospels of the New Testament in Latin.

[52] Dublin Castle was commissioned by king John of England in the 13th century as a defensive fortification for the Norman city of Dublin. Its design was typical Norman courtyard style, with a central square surrounded by a tall defensive wall and supported in each corner by a round tower. The Castle was rebuilt in the 17th century following severe fire, and in the process was converted from a Medieval fortress to a Georgian structure. The only trace of the original medieval buildings above ground is the Record Tower. Historically, the Castle represented the seat for the British government in Ireland. Since 1922, following Irish Independence, the building has served numerous roles, from a temporary home for the Irish courts to presidential inaugurations and other state functions.

medieval wall and an archway were displayed, and in the process, I learned much about the long history of the complex.

From this part of the city, I sometimes took a shortcut back to my residence via Temple Bar.[53] Though in urban decay at that time with many derelict buildings, there still was much to explore on its streets and alleyways. On Parliament Street I passed by the red bricked building where the *Evening Mail* had been published since the 1820s. This was one of the many publishing and printing houses in the area. Most famous among them was the Faulkner firm that published the works of Jonathan Swift and printed the wordbook for Handel's *Messiah*, performed for the first time at the nearby Neal's music hall in April 1742.[54] Cultural activities were synonymous with Temple Bar through the centuries. In search of books, I would stroll along to Temple Bar Square in the hopes of finding bargains, since the street bookstalls were no longer there. As I browsed through the book carts, I imagined seeing a Joycean character searching for his pawned works, as in *Ulysses*. Continuing to explore the quarter, I came upon the historic 17th century Smock Alley Theatre. Though closed then, I learned of its many productions, including Oliver Goldsmith's *She Stoops to Conquer*. In addition to cultural activities, small businesses and entrepreneurs thrived in Temple Bar through the ages. This could be seen from its period buildings along the cobbled streets. Of those, the ones I especially liked were the Queen Anne shop fronts with the Latin inscription which translated to, "Judge us by our actions". Treasures galore were to be found in Temple Bar, such as the 1820s Palace Bar, a historic literary centre on Fleet Street, leaving much to see on future visits. Exiting at Merchant's Arch, I would head towards the Ha'penny Bridge to cross the Liffy

---

[53] It is documented that Dublin's Temple Bar was named after the London Temple Bar, where the medieval toll-gate into London was located. Both Temple Bars have streets in their region bearing similar names, such as Temple, Essex, and Fleet. Dublin's Temple Bar was built on reclaimed land in the 17th century. Its history is deeply rooted with creativity, entrepreneurship, small businesses, and culture. Today, it is best known for its trendy nightlife of clubs, bars, and restaurants, making it a popular tourist attraction.
[54] Jonathan Swift was a foremost prose satirist in the English language (1667 -1745).

in the direction of the Four Courts, encountering a few beggars along the way.[55]

During those same years my sister Francie was also in Dublin, studying midwifery at the National Maternity Hospital located in Holles Street. To visit her, I frequently walked round trip from the Four Courts, a distance of about six miles. Along the way, I passed by Merrion Square with its rows of red brick Georgian townhouses, known for their colourful doors of red, blue, yellow and green.[56] Many notable personalities lived in the square, including Oscar Wilde at #1, Daniel O'Connell at #52 and William Butler Yeats at #82 among others, indicated by the plaques affixed on the doors. Continuing on my walk, I next passed the stately Shelbourne Hotel with its ornate façade.[57] The hotel had an inviting lounge, where I often enjoyed afternoon tea with friends or rendezvoused with dates for an evening out. Arriving at Holles Street, I joined my sister in her shared room at the nurses' quarter of the hospital. Plugging in an electric kettle for tea, Francie served it together with supplies she kept in the room. Several of her nursing colleagues joined us, where we sat around chattering and snacking for hours. One of the nurses in the group was anxious to meet a husband at that time. In her search, she conducted a survey from patients in the maternity ward asking, "Where did you meet your husband Mrs?" Sharing her findings with us, the information gathered was not ideal since it depended on the patients' mood swings either before or after giving birth.

Most of the conversation, however, centred around hospital life, from the matron and doctors to the head nurses and the staff. It all seemed so alien to

---

[55] The Ha'penny Bridge was built in the early 1800s to replace a ferry system for crossing the River Liffey. This pedestrian bridge was originally called the Wellington Bridge after the Dublin-born Duke of Wellington. Later, it was renamed the Liffey Bridge, which remains its official name. It is, however, more commonly known as the Ha'penny Bridge, referring to the toll charged to match that of the replaced ferries. In my day, the bridge was run down and painted black but in recent years, it has been refurbished and restored to its original white colour.

[56] Merrion Square is one of Dublin's finest squares. It is home to the National Gallery, the National History Museum and Leinster House, the Irish seat of government, which was originally built as a palace for the then Duke of Leinster in 1745.

[57] Built in the early 1800s, the Shelbourne Hotel has a rich history. British troops occupied its rooms during the Easter Rising of 1916. Later in 1922, the Irish Constitution was drafted in room #112, renamed the Constitution Room, under the leadership of Michael Collins.

me and helped to convince me that I had chosen a more appropriate career path for myself to match my given talents.

Dublin City exposed me to glamour and style with its beauty parlours and sophisticated shops. As a young woman, I became hooked on fashion and elegance. This led me to Grafton Street, one of the top commercial locations in the city, offering a variety of trendy shops.[58] Among them was and still is, Brown Thomas, Dublin's most prestigious department store. It was there where I first encountered high fashion by continental and Irish designers. Browsing through the display racks, I would dream of owning and wearing such style, should riches ever come my way. On the ground floor stood the cosmetic counters, presenting brand named makeup, creams and perfumes. It was fun to walk among them and sample the promotions while listening to the beauty artists pitch their product lines. At times they offered free facials, which I took advantage of. Seated on the high stool next to the cosmetic

counter, I watched and learned as the beautician described each application. Then, drawing a sketch with painted highlights, she handed me the outline together with product samples in the hopes of gaining a new customer. For me, this was truly an introduction to the allure

of the city and an awakening for the country girl. In addition to vogue, this section of the city had several specialty shops offering Irish tweeds, knits and

---

[58] The street was named after Henry Fitzroy, the first Duke of Grafton, and the son of Charles 2nd of England. Established in the 18th century, it housed the Whyte Academy, a British grammar school attended by prominent citizens, including Thomas Moore, Robert Emmet and the Duke of Wellington.

wools. The market for these traditional Irish manufactured goods, including the Aran sweater, was well established, and much sought after by the tourists. Also prominent were leather and skin merchandise. Because it was considered fashionable and practical for the winter, I purchased one such garment, a sheepskin coat. It has proven to be a life-time investment that I can't get rid of, since it still hangs in my closet, weighing a tonne, as a reminder of my Dublin spree.

On the opposite side on Grafton Street was Bewley's Café, an iconic Dublin landmark, established in the early 1900s on the site of the Whyte Academy. The café was inviting, with its open fireplaces, mahogany panelling, and magnificent stained-glass windows.[59] Known for its high-quality coffee, tea blends and confectioneries, I often got together there with friends for a snack. Inside, we joined the Bewley bakery line with our trays to make our selections. From the many choices of buns, including cherry and almond to sticky raisin, I sampled each on different visits. Having made our selections, my friends and I routinely sought a corner spot next to a window where we placed our food on a marble-topped table and sat on the bentwood chairs to enjoy our treats and our meet up. Apart from the dining, the café seemed to

---

[59] Designed by Harry Clarke, a famous Irish stained-glass artist and book illustrator of the early 1900s.

foster newspaper reading. Whether borrowed from the café racks or brought in by the patrons, newspapers were ubiquitous around the café. The readers all appeared to have a great appetite for news, and Bewley's offered the perfect setting for a good read while sipping on their world-class coffee or tea.

Leaving the café and my pals, I very often headed towards Saint Stephen's Green, located at the top of Grafton Street.[60] At one of its four entrances stood the Fusiliers Arch, where I passed through to enter the Green.[61] This well laid out public park, with its exotic plants and large lake with waterfall, offered much to see. Walking along its pedestrian pathways I passed numerous memorials and monuments dedicated to Irish leaders, artists, and to wars. On these walks, I always made a point of stopping by the scented flower gardens, or the lake to watch the ducks being fed as a reminder of my family's farm in Mayo. It was common to rent a folding chair in the park or sit on a bench which I sometimes did to contemplate my

surroundings and watch the world go by, making it a perfect ending of a visit to Dublin's south side.

Living in Dublin City was an enriching experience for me, with its famous landmarks, stately buildings and magnificent architecture. I took pleasure in walking its streets, crossing its bridges, visiting its ancient treasures, sharing its culture and shopping in its markets and stores. From clothing boutiques to beauty parlours, I followed the latest trends and indulged in the fads, with the intent of dressing up to look attractive for the dances. Attending the dances around Dublin, however, was very different than at home. Apart from the Metropole Ballroom, many were segmented by interest groups, such

---

[60] St. Stephen's Green was designed in the 1800s by William Sheppard featuring a gate at each of its four corners, and a lake with a waterfall in its centre.
[61] The Fusiliers Arch is a memorial to the Royal Dublin Fusiliers who fought in South Africa in the second Boer War,1899-1902.

as tennis and rugby clubs or by professional groups for engineers and for veterinarians. While they offered choice and diversity, for me they were more formal, less personal, and less fun than those around home. While I attended many and enjoyed the encounters, transitioning socially from rural life to city life was an adjustment.

# 38

# Home Sick

Staying connected with family and friends meant frequent exchanges by mail. In writing these letters, we took pride in our stationery choice and our penmanship, and in displaying our command of the English language. Planning a trip home was always elating. For weeks, I anticipated the thrill of seeing everyone around home again, as I counted the days remaining. I shopped in the city for family gifts to take along, usually practical household items that were needed, like dishes, glassware and the occasional ornament. Of those, the ones Mam most cherished were the two complementary dog statues, which she placed on the kitchen mantle as a reminder of the family dogs, Bruno and Victor. The journey to the West took an entire day by train, as it stopped in each town along the way dropping off passengers and packages. I frequently travelled by train, catching it at Westland Row station in Dublin. On board, I treated myself to tea and sandwiches in the dining car, set up with white linen tablecloths, delph and silverware. As the train chugged and whistled along, the tea in my cup moved accordingly, splashing around and making it difficult to drink. From the train window I could view the green fields with cattle grazing and farmhouses in the distance. Sitting there and staring out, a feeling of tranquillity and peace would come over me knowing that I was on my way home.

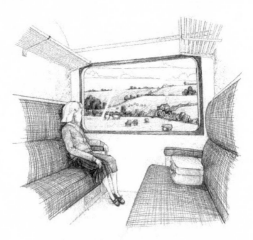

Arriving at Ballina train station at the end of my journey, I would see the same familiar hackney drivers, Mr. Hughes and Mr. Battle, standing there looking for customers. It seemed as though they were cut in stone, since they never changed in appearance with their distinct opposite body types, emphasized by the hat and cap worn respectively by each. Occasionally I hired them but preferred to walk the three-mile distance to Caltra Village, carrying my small suitcase as I passed the neighbours' homes along the way. The air had a recognisable smell of burning turf, causing a deep calmness to creep over me as I came closer to our house.

In my day, the train from Dublin to the West was limited to one a day, with no service on Sundays and Holy Days. Missing the noon departure time, meant finding an alternative means of travel. Though not ideal, hitching a ride was an accepted and common option. It entailed catching a city bus to the end of its line, and from there, trying one's luck. Once in a while I, together with pals, resorted to this mode of travel. The flow of traffic from the city was steady, though most cars were going short distances. This meant watching for cars with foreign licence plates since they were usually visitors travelling longer distances.

A perfect target for us were the Great Britain (GB) licence plates, knowing that these tourists were generous with their lifts. As passengers in their cars, we discovered that many were Irish themselves, on holidays from their jobs in England. They told us about life across the pond, with all of the work to be had in the building trade. We learned of their roles as foremen supervising teams of workers. Some spoke with an English accent which we could hardly understand. This left us wondering how so many of them could be foremen and if the accent, or *twang* as we called it, was a prerequisite for job promotion or for upward mobility in general. They appeared to have lots of spending money, sometimes treating us to a drink or a snack along the way. It was marvellous to meet fellow citizens by chance and to experience their generosity and pride in their work. Were they among the *Forgotten Irish* who toiled abroad, I pondered, sending home their hard-earned money to help keep Ireland afloat during the 1950s?

*"Oh, Mary, this London's a wonderful sight*
*With people here working by day and by night.*
*They don't sow potatoes, nor barley, nor wheat*
*But there's gangs of them diggin' for gold in the street ... "*

*The Mountains of Mourne* by William Percy French (1854-1920)

Once I reached Ballina after hitchhiking, I generally hung around until the train arrived, thus letting Mam believe that I had travelled by train, since she objected to hitching rides. My homecomings were very special for Mam, lifting her spirits and visiting several of our neighbours. There was no set agenda for our visits, we just decided for ourselves and were always welcomed. Dropping in on one elderly man, Willie Melvin, who lived with his two mature sons, I heard the remark, "There must be an awful sight of *aul* motorcars up there in Dublin," to which I replied, "Fierce sight indeed." They shared their humorous outlook on modern lifestyles and changing trends, keeping Mam and me highly amused during our visit. Content with their small farm and house, they had no desire to venture afar. Their sister, Maureen, had a different outlook however. A close family friend, she followed in my sister's footsteps to London as a student nurse, followed by a nursing career in the U.S. Maureen's cheerful disposition was her strength for adventure.

As mentioned in previous chapters, the automobile was still a novelty that few Irish families could afford. It was considered a significant step up from the one-horse carriage that prosperous families still used and from the bicycle that the majority then used. The ubiquitous bicycle came in all shapes and sizes with carrier and basket for multiple uses. We learned to repair flat tires, oil squeaky wheels and keep lights operational.

Over time, the automobile took over, for better or worse. Along with remarkable convenience, speed and comfort came pollution, traffic, and accidents. At first, we did not understand the resulting destructive impact on our environment and on our lives. Seventy years later, we now deal with uncontrollable fires, floods and storms, contributions from the carbon emissions of the automobile. With curious irony, we witness the return of our old friend, the bicycle, that we had discarded years ago. Today, it can be found in cities around the world as an important means of transportation. This is true for Ireland, which has experienced a renaissance of cycling.

Stopping by another house while on holidays at home, Mam and I were served *poitín*, a drink that I had never tasted before. Not being much of a drinker, I would throw the moonshine from my glass into the fire next to me once the host turned her back. The resulting flames caused the neighbour to question what was going wrong with her fire. Continuing to refill my glass, she could only conclude that Dublin had turned me into an alcoholic.

The next highlight of my homecoming was always a return to the dance halls with my friends. This provided an opportunity for me to wear my trendy dresses and accessories that I had purchased in Dublin. At these dances, I also could flaunt my chic hairstyle together with my makeup as demonstrated at the cosmetic counters on Grafton Street. The city had changed my persona and the country ballrooms allowed me to show off my in-vogue glamour. Word would get around that I was home. Not knowing which ballroom or dance I planned to attend, one admirer, named Cathal, checked out a few until he found me. Seeing that I was already on the floor dancing, Cathal would tap my shoulder with a request to hold the next dance. He and I had a stormy intermittent relationship that lasted a few years. Blonde and blue-eyed and of medium build, Cathal's appeal was his friendly personality and sharp wit, ideally suited for the bar and grocery business that he owned and operated in Ballina. It was fun to connect with him and with others during my holidays at home.

For the return trip to Dublin, I had different options, since several local businessmen drove to the city delivering and collecting supplies. One such man, Ned McCann, was very generous with his lifts. Driving a large lorry for a Guinness distributor, Ned travelled weekly to Dublin. His lorry was high up from the ground, almost requiring a stepladder to reach it. Added to the difficulty was my tight skirt and high heels, which was the dress code for women then, as wearing slacks was considered unladylike. Perched on a high seat next to Ned, we chatted along the way, keeping our voices high to offset the noise of the lorry. This was an all-day journey, and at its end both my voice and my ears needed a rest. Approaching Dublin, I noted the yellow lights of the city with their cold glow and contrasted them with the warm flame from the turf fire at home. Once again back in the city, I readied myself to resume my duties at the hotel. Then, stepping cautiously down from the high lorry lest I catch my skirt or nylons in the descent, I said farewell to Ned as I slipped a pound note into his hand in the hope that he would treat himself to a pint in the pub that evening.

My sister Francie and me.

Part Eleven

# Emigration

# 39

# The Camelot Era

In 1960 John F. Kennedy was elected as President of the United States. All of Ireland was proud of their native son, and anyone with a Kennedy name made claim to his lineage.[62] His picture hung in every home, next to that of Pope John himself. Tourists flocked to the Kennedy homestead in Wexford to meet with his confirmed cousin, Mary Ryan, and to have a photo taken next to her. For the Irish, America was a wonderland, all powerful and wealthy.

Many American people visited our shores in search of their ancestors. We referred to them as *Yanks*, and from them we learned about the greatness of *The States*, the land of opportunity and the almighty dollar. Some of them displayed their wealth by buying up lands, building new homes and establishing businesses in Ireland. As tourists, they sought the comforts they

---

[62] This was a common trait among the Irish. They admired the rich and famous, and claim them as a relative. Many indeed were related, given the migration patterns of the Irish. In addition to President Kennedy, other U.S. presidents had traceable Irish lineage. They include Ford, Reagan and Biden. Even Obama came to Ireland in search of his roots. While there, he learned that O'Bama was the correct spelling of his family name. In his search he found an eighth cousin, called Henry, better known today as Henry the VIII.

were used to in *The States* by staying at the best hotels where their expectations could be satisfied. One such tourist who was staying at the Downhill Hotel, photographed a group of us children as we walked home from Mass. From a copy he sent to each one of us, we learned that he was Edward J. Cronin, Secretary of the Commonwealth of Massachusetts. For years thereafter, he continued to send us Christmas cards, bearing the stamp of the Commonwealth. This important connection encouraged some of us to believe that we too could achieve fame and riches in that distant land across the ocean.

*"In the year of our Lord 1806, we set sail from the fair Cobh of Cork.*
*We were bound far away with a cargo of bricks for the fine City Hall*
*Of New York ..."*

*The Irish Rover* by Joseph Crofts (1820-1878)

When I decided to leave Ireland, my intention was to spend just one year abroad. I was influenced by the stories I had heard from returning emigrants who described the marvels of the cities with their tall buildings, bright lights and fast pace. As a young person, I wanted to experience these sights for myself. America was enjoying an all-time boom at that time, while Ireland remained poor with no revolutionary developments. Mass emigration continued with political challenges for change. The need for greater prosperity became the objective and concern for the next generation, as suggested in the closing sentiments of the documentary *Ireland, The Tear and the Smile.*

While I was comfortable with my life and job in Dublin, my wanderlust prevailed. When I told my hotel manager about my leaving, he was disappointed, since he had plans to increase my responsibilities and we had a wonderful working relationship. This caused me to question my decision to leave. Standing at the bus stop across from the hotel on that final day, I contemplated my surroundings with uncertainty. This was compounded during the following week at home, with Mam refusing to talk to me and friends dropping by our house to wish me well. Among them was my schoolmate Annie who cycled the round-trip journey from her village in Whitestream to say good-bye. She, together with other acquaintances, appeared content in their world, unlike me. Why did I believe that one must leave Ireland to better oneself, to achieve greatness, to generate wealth? Was I misled by the returning Irish who flaunted their money and bragged about life abroad? Why had Ireland failed its youth? I had witnessed the distress of family separations, the tears and the sorrows, the mass exodus, the longing for home. I was facing the same fate. But no, I was only going away for one year to broaden my perspective, or so I convinced myself. With the way paved and my U.S. sponsorship and working visa in hand, there was no turning back. I took my chances on exploring the unknown and on satisfying my ambitions in America.

# 40

# Coming Full Circle

Today, as I visit my parent's gravesite in League Cemetery in the town of Ballina, the surroundings look so familiar to me. Standing here, I recall the first time I set foot at the site. I was then a four-year old child attending my father's burial. The landscape has changed little, except for the expansion of the grounds, now segmented into the old and the new plots. As I walk around, I recognise so many names displayed on various tombstones. They are those of the neighbours that I grew up with in Caltra Village. I stop and visit with a few and find it reassuring to see them resting there next to each other in peace, as they did in life.

As I exit the cemetery, I see the tombstone of my godparents, Jim and Joan Rafter, right next to the gate. I know then that I have returned home to the place where my roots are firmly planted, a place that, in some ways, I never truly left. It is indeed *My Ireland.*

CPSIA information can be obtained
at www.ICGtesting.com
Printed in the USA
LVHW030958170323
741844LV00003B/111

9 781739 872533